LOGIC
An Outline

by ROBERT SHARVY

About the Author

1. Present position: Professor of Philosophy and Head of Philosophy Department, Lake Forest College.
2. Consultant on philosophy for American Educator Encyclopedia; author of articles on "Fallacies" and on "Logic and Rhetoric."

About the Book

1. A concise yet comprehensive treatment of the materials covered in the standard "Introduction to Logic" course.
2. The topics arranged to begin with the exact procedures of deduction and end with a study of language and non-formal fallacies.
3. Unity attained by focusing all of the material on the problem of evaluating arguments.
4. Numerous and cumulative exercises that allow the book to be used much like a programmed text in logic.

LITTLEFIELD, ADAMS & CO.

TOTOWA, NEW JERSEY

LOGIC: AN OUTLINE

by

ROBERT SHARVY

PROFESSOR OF PHILOSOPHY
LAKE FOREST COLLEGE

1970

LITTLEFIELD, ADAMS & CO.

Totowa, New Jersey

PRINTED IN THE UNITED STATES OF AMERICA

Preface

The primary purpose of this outline is to serve as a text for the standard semester course generally called "Introduction to Logic." Because of its conciseness and its outline form as well as the generous number of exercises, it should also prove useful as a supplement to any of the other texts currently in use.

With so many logic texts already available, a new entry in the field presumably needs some justification. Two convictions have guided the writing of the present book: 1) Applied logic is primarily an art. As a consequence of this position, the emphasis is placed on the ability to evaluate arguments. The scientific principles that underlie logic are introduced only as they are used in the analysis of arguments. Every topic in the text is focused directly on the problem of evaluating arguments. 2) A logic text can be brief. The brevity is accomplished by tightly tying all of the material to the concept of argument, and further, by excluding material that belongs properly to the *philosophy* of logic. After stating and explaining the principles and rules used to evaluate arguments, an opening is left by the text for the instructor to give a theoretical justification of the principles according to his own philosophical orientation.

One further departure from common practice consists in the organization of the text. The arrangement is such that the student begins with the very exact material of the categorical syllogism and ends with the rather "loose" material characteristic of language and fallacies. This arrangement has the advantage of implanting early the idea that the subject matter of a logic course is logic and that logic is a rigorous study. Instead of the customary "bogging down in semantics," a beginning is made with the artificial standard forms and then these are used to handle ordinary discourse. Semantics and fallacies are introduced as a unit at the end of the book as a sort of "mopping-up tool" for the material that cannot be handled by the principles of deduction and induction.

I should like to express my appreciation to Professor Douglas

Morgan for his reading of an earlier version and his many helpful suggestions. A special note of thanks must go to Professor John Worley who used the earlier version in several of his logic classes and made numerous valuable criticisms.

R. S.

TABLE OF CONTENTS

PART III: INDUCTION

PART IV: SEMANTICS

Chapter I

INTRODUCTION

The word "logical" is used frequently in everyday discourse, yet for the most part without claim of much precision. One person may remark that another person's statement is "not very logical" and mean only by this that the person's statement, in one way or another, "is not reasonable." The purpose of this introductory chapter is to define logic, indicate its usefulness, and present a preliminary exploration of its major divisions and basic concepts.

1. Definition of logic

It is customary to define a subject by stating the general field of its study (its genus) and then indicating what the specific concern is within this general field (its species). Following this procedure, logic can be defined as the study of the rules of correct argument.

a) GENUS OF LOGIC: The general field of the study of logic is argument. This statement might seem clear enough on the surface but a word of warning must be injected. The word "argument" is not being used in its everyday sense of quarreling or bickering; the word "argument" is a technical term in logic.

1. DEFINITION OF ARGUMENT: By argument is meant discourse in which it is claimed that one or more of the sentences are evidence for another sentence called the conclusion. The notion is that one sentence "follows from" another sentence or sentences. From the point of view of the psychological process involved, the situation would be one where reasoning occurs or where an inference is being made. An example of an argument would be: "Iron rusts. Guns are made of iron. Therefore, guns rust."

2. <u>DEFINITION OF ASSERTION</u>: In contrast to argument is discourse where there is merely an assertion or a series of assertions with no claim that evidence is being presented for a conclusion. A crude example might be: "New York is a large city. Paris is in Europe. Russia is large." These assertions are nothing more than assertions—there is no connection between them. We might believe any one of them or all of them but no evidence is presented for any of them. We could call such discourse "reasonable" but we should not call it logical in the strict sense.

b) <u>SPECIES OF LOGIC:</u> Within the general field of argument the specific concern of logic is with the problem of correctness. The logician is not concerned with describing the brain processes involved in reasoning, nor with the problem of whether particular sentences in an argument are true, but instead, he focuses on the normative problem of establishing rules for correctly getting from the evidence to the conclusion. Assuming the evidence is true, would it make the conclusion true or probably true? We may not know whether all guns are made of iron, but we can know that if they are and if iron rusts, then all guns must rust. Many times we must reason without knowing whether our facts are true but we do want our reasoning to be correct.

2. The value of logic

Argument occupies a dominant position in all human discourse. Perhaps most human discourse involves reasoning of some kind. The student who says, "I am intelligent because I received an 'A' on the examination" is reasoning and consequently presenting an argument. He is claiming that the fact of his "A" is evidence for the truth of the conclusion that he is intelligent. Of course a person can argue correctly without a course in logic but at the same time, studying logic should improve whatever reasoning ability a person does possess.

a) <u>PERCEPTIONS OF CORRECTNESS SHARPENED:</u> It seems reasonable to say that doing many exercises will help build the habit of arguing correctly. Many arguments are so simple that they can be evaluated in one intuitive sweep; however, without practice this intuitive sweep is apt to come up with the wrong answer. Is the following argument correct? "Only faculty members can use this washroom and Mr. Smith is a faculty member, hence he can use this washroom." The argument looks good to the untutored mind but in fact it is incorrect.

b) MECHANICAL EVALUATION OF LENGTHY ARGUMENTS: There are some arguments with many complicated sentences as evidence. It is as difficult for the human mind to evaluate such arguments as it would be to handle long arithmetic problems without paper and pencil. If the evidence in the following argument is true, does it make the conclusion true? Could you defend your answer? "If R has information about the stock he will be called on to testify. If he is not called on to testify he will go on vacation. If he goes on vacation, he will spend money. He has no information about the stock nor does he know anyone who does. Therefore he will spend money." With the aid of rules of logic these complicated arguments can be evaluated easily and quickly.

c) AVOIDANCE OF OBVIOUS FALLACIES: An acquaintance with some of the most glaring fallacies will serve as a kind of inoculation against them. No student of logic would ever accept the following argument: "The biggest companies in the world seek out the best equipped men for their top jobs, so why shouldn't the universities go after the best athletic talent?"

3. The parts of an argument

The fundamental elements of an argument are propositions, and these function either as premises or as the conclusion. An indication of how a given proposition is functioning is usually given by certain clue words that connect up the propositions of an argument.

a) DEFINITION OF PROPOSITION: A proposition is what a declarative sentence means. According to this usage, the two sentences "The dog is brown" and "*Le chien est brun*" express one proposition since they have the same meaning. Also, the two sentences "all men are mortal" and "no men are immortal" express one proposition. It also follows from this definition that sentences such as "Open the door," and "Are you awake?" do not express propositions because they are not declarative sentences. Logic is concerned with propositions and not with sentences, except as they express propositions, because inference is a connection between meanings and not between marks on a piece of paper.

b) PREMISES AND CONCLUSION: In an argument, the proposition or propositions that form the evidence for the inference are called the premise, or premises, and the proposition to which the inference is made is called the conclusion. Before considering whether an argument is correct or incorrect, it is obvious that a prior step consists in identifying a piece of discourse as an argument. If treating a piece of discourse as an argument results in observing a correct argument, then presumably an argument is being presented. However, if treating a piece of discourse as an argument results in observing an incorrect argument, how is it possible to tell whether an argument is intended? How do we know that a person is claiming that one proposition follows from other propositions when it actually does not follow?

c) CLUE WORDS: There are certain clue words that indicate premises and conclusion and hence the existence of an argument. These clue words have been invented for the English language to indicate inference and hence argument. The words "therefore," "thus," "hence," "consequently," "so," usually indicate an argument and when they indicate an argument, they always precede the conclusion. The words "because," "for," "since," usually indicate an argument and when they indicate an argument, they always precede a premise. Frequently the word "and" is used to connect the premises of an argument. When no clue words are present and the discourse would present an incorrect argument if it were treated as an argument, then the only recourse will be to sensitivity to language usage. If the discourse bears some resemblance to a correct argument, then it is likely that an argument is intended. For example, the following is probably an argument, albeit of course, fallacious: "Liberals are against segregation. Communists are against segregation. Liberals are communists."

4. Pseudo-arguments

A complication arises when clue words occur even though there is no argument. Such pieces of discourse can be called pseudo-arguments because they have the appearance of being arguments but are really assertions. There are two such exceptions to the argumentative use of clue words that are important enough to note.

a) <u>CAUSAL EXPLANATIONS</u>: One type of pseudo-argument is a causal explanation such as "grass is green because it has chlorophyll." An argument is something that can be assessed by logic, *i.e.*, by considering the evidential bearing of the premises on the conclusion. The example above is not stating evidence for a conclusion that "grass is green," but instead is asserting a cause for the fact that grass is green. We know grass is green and are stating what makes it that way. There is a difference between giving reasons for believing a fact and reasons for the existence of a fact. The word "because" is ambiguous and in the example cited is intended to assert a causal connection rather than to introduce evidence for a conclusion. This assertion might be phrased as "chlorophyll is the cause of grass being green." Whether the assertion of causal connection is correct or not is a matter for experimentation and not for logical analysis. If the question were asked, "How do we know grass is green?", it would not be sensible to respond with "it has chlorophyll." If the discourse had been worded "grass has chlorophyll, therefore, grass is green," then there would presumably be an argument. Normally, however, people do not present arguments for a proposition that is a matter of immediate sense observation as is the case for "grass is green."

b) <u>REPEATED ASSERTIONS</u>: A second type of pseudo-argument is the repeated assertion. Frequently something like the following is heard: "The *Republicrats* are the best party. They always have been the best party and always will be the best party. Therefore, it is clear that the *Republicrats* are the best party." As all advertisers know, the effect of such repetition is conviction, and from this it is but a short step to the hazy notion that evidence has been heard. This is not the case. Two or more assertions do not necessarily make an argument. In a real argument, the conclusion does not merely repeat one of the premises.

5. Two kinds of real arguments

Within the area of argument proper there are two types, each of which takes its own special tests for correctness.

a) <u>DEDUCTIVE ARGUMENT</u>: In a deductive argument the claim is made that if the premises are true, the conclusion must be true. The conclusion is claimed to follow necessarily from the premises—the premises imply the conclusion—it is impossible for the premises to be true and the conclusion to be false. An example would be: "Since everyone in the class will get an 'A' and John is in the class, John will get an 'A'." The basis for the claim is that the very meaning of the premises makes it necessary for the conclusion to be true; if we understand what it means to say that John is in a class and everyone in the class gets an "A," then we will know that John must get an "A."

b) <u>INDUCTIVE ARGUMENT</u>: An inductive argument is one in which the claim is made that if the premises are true, it is more or less probable—not absolutely certain—that the conclusion is true. The conclusion is claimed to follow probably from the premises—it is not likely that the premises are true and the conclusion false. An example is: "John has received an 'A' in 100 hours of school work, therefore he probably will get an 'A' in this course." The word "probable" must be used or understood before the conclusion of an inductive argument because the premise is a fact known through experience and experience is never "all in." It is possible that the sun will not rise tomorrow.

6. The meaning of validity

In a well-constructed inductive argument, if the premises are true, the conclusion has a degree of probability higher than that given by the toss of a coin. The example of induction given above is a case in point and such an argument will be called justified. When the conclusion of a deductive argument actually does follow necessarily from the premises as in the example of deduction, then the relation of implication is present and the argument is called valid. It should be emphasized that validity and justification are not defined in terms of the premises actually being true. Clearly we are in no position in a logic class to determine the truth of premises and hence to evaluate the over-all soundness of an argument. So far as logic is concerned, all of the premises in argument are considered as true. The premises being taken as true, the question is "do the premises make the conclusion true or probably true?" That this question is important can be seen when the following argument is considered: "All Texans are mortal and all Americans are mortal, hence all Americans are Texans." We not only want truth, we want well-reasoned truth.

a) VALID ARGUMENTS: A valid argument can have various combinations of true and false propositions. There can be a valid argument with all false propositions such as "all men are fish and all fish are birds, therefore all men are birds," or there can be a valid argument with false premises and a true conclusion, such as "all men are fish and all fish are rational beings, therefore all men are rational beings." The point is that the conclusion in each of these cases follows necessarily from the premises—if the premises were true, the conclusion would necessarily be true. The only situation that cannot exist is one in which there is a valid argument with true premises and a false conclusion. This is a self-contradictory notion because what is meant by validity is good reasoning, *i.e.,* reasoning that will produce a true conclusion if one starts with true premises.

b) INVALID ARGUMENTS: An invalid argument can have any kind of combination of true and false propositions. For example, the following argument has all true propositions but it is invalid: "all Texans are mortal and all Americans are mortal, therefore all Texans are Americans." In this case we just happen to know that the conclusion is true; the conclusion is not validated on the basis of an inference from the premises. The evidence that all Texans are mortal and all Americans are mortal does not make the conclusion true any more than the premises that all dogs are animals and all cats are animals prove that all dogs are cats.

7. Summary

We have seen that logic is concerned with the formulation of rules for the evaluation of arguments. In the material to come, the early chapters consider rules for evaluating deductive arguments and the later chapters will handle rules for evaluating inductive arguments. The exposition will be completed by a final chapter on arguments that are so bad that rules are not required for their evaluation; it is simply a matter of becoming familiar with the various types of such horrendous arguments. However, before going into the evaluation of arguments there is the preliminary stage of being sure that an argument is present and being aware of the conclusion that is intended. An understanding of these two points is the chief aim of the present chapter and of the first two exercises.

EXERCISE #1: ARGUMENT

Working with verbal puzzles is an excellent method of discovering what is meant by reasoning and argumentation. The problem posed by a puzzle is not merely the statement of the answer but an argument in which the answer is the conclusion and in which it is proved. Try solving some of these puzzles by constructing an argument in which your answer is proved. If you enjoy puzzles, see "Introduction to Logic" by I. Copi where some of the following puzzles and many more can be found.

1. In a certain kingdom all missionaries only tell the truth and all slaves only tell lies. Three strangely dressed men came before the king. The king asked the first, "What are you—slave or missionary?" The first mumbled something the king could not hear. The king then asked the second, "What did he say?" The second replied, "He says he's a slave." The king asked the third man if the second was telling the truth and he replied "Yes."

   Who are you certain are slaves? Who are you certain are missionaries?

2. There are five top hats in a room; three white ones and two black ones. Three men enter the room, see the hats, are blindfolded, and sit down in chairs that are arranged one behind the other. Three hats are chosen at random and a hat placed on each man's head. The blindfolds are removed, and without looking behind, each man is asked what color hat he has on. The last man and the man sitting in the middle both admit they do not know. The man sitting in front (so he has seen no hats at all) stands up and says he has a .... hat on.

   What color was his hat?

3. Six members of a mixed hockey team are Mr. A, Mr. B, Mr. C, Mrs. D, Miss E, and Miss F. The positions they occupy are center, right wing, left wing, right defense, left defense, and goalie, though not necessarily in that order. Mr. A is a bachelor. Mr. B is 20 years old. Miss E is the left defense's step-sister. Mr. C is the center's neighbor. The right wing is the center's grandson. The left wing is the son-in-law of the right defense.

Who plays each position?

4. You have twelve golf balls numbered 1 through 12, one of which is defective in that it weighs more or less than the others. They are identical in every other way. You have only a set of balance scales which do not tell weight, but will balance when equal weights are put on each side.

The problem is: how could we in three weighings determine which golf ball is defective and whether it is heavier or lighter?

EXERCISE #2: ARGUMENT

For each of the following pieces of discourse: 1) If there is no argument, write assertion. 2) If there is an argument, a) underline or write out the conclusion; b) identify the argument as deductive or inductive; c) make an estimate as to the correctness of the argument.

1. No dog is a cat because all dogs bark and no cat barks.
2. On the basis of an examination of the testing scores of one half of the freshman class and finding them all above the national average, it appears likely that all of the freshmen are above the national average on such tests.
3. Smith was notified in 1954 that he was being fired because of his close association with individuals "reliably reported to be communists" and because of his contacts with Friends of America, an organization on the Attorney General's subversive list.
4. Radio helped football and so does television but each means of communication must be controlled.
5. All communists believe in equality and all democrats believe in equality, therefore, all democrats are communists.

6. The teacher must be at home sick because he missed his classes today and this has never happened before. Also, yesterday in class he sneezed and coughed and appeared to be in bad shape.

7. To require a man to beg for a trial on a charge of murder requires too much of human nature. Conversely, to keep him in suspense for twenty years approaches the inhuman.

8. Ninety per cent of the members are for the resolution. No doubt about it. Absolutely none at all.

9. My head aches because I studied too much last night.

10. "I think that in November he will win by the biggest vote ever given anyone in this state. To win here a national candidate must appeal to the independent voter, and Ike has an appeal that is just out of this world."

11. Since no good person is a person who likes brutality and all bullies are persons who like brutality, no good person is a bully.

12. If you spend a great deal of time studying logic you will get a good grade. If you don't spend a great deal of time studying logic you will have much fun. Since you either will spend a great deal of time studying logic or you won't, it follows that you will either get a good grade or you will have much fun.

13. Since all of the red-heads I have known have had bad tempers, it is likely that all red-heads have bad tempers.

14. "Even as a lovely flower, so fair and pure thou art. I gaze on thee and sadness comes stealing o'er my heart."

15. Mr. Henry has asked me to inform all of you that the state's attorney's office is making an inquiry. The auditor's policy of permitting newspapers to examine specific records upon request has been suspended.

16. Since aspirin "A" dissolves faster in a glass of water than does aspirin "B," it follows that aspirin "A" will dissolve faster in the human stomach than will aspirin "B."

17. The present jury system should be thoroughly investigated and then perhaps recommendations can be made that will result in a great improvement.

18. For all arguments, underline the conclusion and indicate

whether the argument is valid or invalid. If invalid, state why.

19. The U.N. is a failure. It has not succeeded in doing anything worthwhile. This can clearly be demonstrated. It follows from this that the U.N. is a complete washout.

20. If this isn't a terrible exercise, then I don't know a terrible one when I see one.

21. Why were these special branches of learning called "natural"? Not because they were more natural, in the conventional sense, than any other; but because they were regarded as being especially concerned with nature.

22. Your editorial of March 1, purporting to disprove Eisenhower's favoritism toward big business is unconvincing. Your chart represents composites for all corporate profit and shows a decline in aggregate corporation profits under Eisenhower. Should you represent graphically the profits of the 100 largest corporations you would have an entirely different picture.

23. Since no totalitarians are democrats, no totalitarians are people with sound moral views on politics, for all democrats are people with sound moral views on politics.

24. Since all diamonds are valuable, no diamonds can be picked from trees, because no valuable thing can be picked from a tree.

25. Class attendance should be abolished because such a system restricts the freedom of the students.

PART I

ARISTOTELIAN LOGIC

By Aristotelian logic is customarily meant the deductive logic of the categorical syllogism. This logic was developed by Aristotle in the fourth century B.C., and up to the nineteenth century it remained almost the sole tool for handling deductive arguments. Toward the end of the last century new systems of logic were introduced, but it still is true that for the purpose of evaluating deductive arguments as they occur in everyday discourse, the logic formulated by Aristotle is a most useful tool. A parallel might be drawn between the relation of the new geometries of the nineteenth century to Euclid, and of the new logics to Aristotle. Though the new geometries have their uses, it is still true that for the geometrical operations of everyday affairs the primary tool is Euclid. The next three chapters will analyze the categorical syllogism according to the following plan: first, the basic forms will be introduced; second, a study will be made of the relations that exist among categorical propositions; third, all of this material will be brought to bear on the evaluation of deductive arguments as they occur in ordinary discourse.

Chapter II

THE CATEGORICAL SYLLOGISM: STANDARD FORMS

The syllogism, a deductive argument in which two premises lead to a conclusion, is one of the commonest forms of argument. It is being used when a person says: "We should hold the party on Saturday night since most of the members want it at that time and the constitution says that a majority vote shall rule." Perhaps most of the time our everyday arguments are not so brief, but when they are not, it may be that syllogisms form a part of our total argument, or our total argument may consist in a series of syllogisms.

1. Kinds of syllogisms

There are different kinds of syllogisms and they are distinguished according to the types of propositions that enter into their construction.

a) THE CATEGORICAL SYLLOGISM: A categorical syllogism is constructed out of three categorical propositions. An example would be: "All mothers are females; no trees are females, therefore, no trees are mothers." The propositions that make up this syllogism are called categorical because each proposition is made up of parts that are terms and not propositions. A categorical proposition cannot be subdivided into further propositions. It should be noted that the premises are frequently joined by the word "and." The study of the categorical syllogism is usually referred to as classical or Aristotelian logic.

b) THE COMPOUND SYLLOGISM: An example of the compound syllogism is: "If John is breathing, then John is alive; John is breathing, therefore, John is alive." When a syllogism has in it one or more compound propositions then it is a compound syllogism. By a compound proposition is meant a proposition that can be subdivided into two or more simple propositions. "If John is breathing, then John is alive," can be divided into "John is breathing" and "John is alive." What is called modern or symbolic logic is primarily a study of the compound syllogism in its various forms.

2. The standard form categorical proposition

We will begin our study of the syllogism with the categorical syllogism, but before doing this there must be a prior study of the categorical proposition. In order to be able to apply the rules of validity to the categorical syllogism in an easy and mechanical manner, it is necessary to have the propositions in what is called "standard form." The following standard form propositions, with the letter name, traditionally given to them, will serve as a model for our discussion:

1.	All girls are flirts.	"A"
2.	No girls are flirts.	"E"
3.	Some girls are flirts.	"I"
4.	Some girls are not flirts.	"O"
5.	Mary is a flirt.	"A"
6.	Mary is not a flirt.	"E"

a) THE PARTS OF A STANDARD FORM CATEGORICAL PROPOSITION: The four parts are: 1) subject; 2) predicate; 3) copula; 4) quantifier.

The subject and predicate terms: In the first four propositions of our model list, we find a relation asserted between the subject term "girls" and the predicate term "flirts." Each of these terms refers to classes of objects, hence we can regard the propositions as asserting a relation between classes of objects. By a class is meant a collection of objects having some characteristic in common, therefore the following will all be names for classes: "girls," "flirts," "boys in this room," "boys who are not afraid of snakes," etc. On the other hand, "red" cannot be a subject or predicate because it does not name a class of objects, though "red things" can function as a subject or predicate. In the case of the last two propositions on our list, the so-called singular propositions, the subject is not a class but it can be treated as a class having only one member.

The copula: The copula in our model list is a form of the present tense of the verb "to be": is—is not; am—am not; are—are not. The function of the copula is to assert a connection between the subject class and the predicate class in a relation of class inclusion or class exclusion. The proposition "all girls are flirts" is including the class of girls in the class of flirts; the proposition "no girls are flirts" is excluding the class of girls from the class of flirts. In similar fashion, propositions 3 and 5 assert class inclusion and propositions 4 and 6 assert class exclusion. Propositions that assert class inclusion are called affirmative while propositions that assert exclusion are called negative. The characteristic of being affirmative or negative is referred to as the "quality" of a proposition.

The quantifier: The part of the proposition that tells how much of the subject term is being referred to is called the quantifier. The only quantifiers that will be used are "all," "no," or "some." Singular propositions will not have a quantifier but they will be mentally regarded as having an "all" in front of them if they are affirmative as "Mary is a flirt" or a "no" before them if they are negative as "Mary is not a flirt."

When the quantifiers refer to the complete subject class then the proposition is called a "universal" proposition. The quantifiers "all" and "no" make this complete reference, hence they are called universal quantifiers. The quantifier "some" only refers to a part of the subject class, and propositions with this quantifier are called particular propositions. In ordinary usage, "some" means anything from a few to many; in order to get greater precision we will take it to mean at least one. In this sense, it will be proper to say that "some men are over seven feet tall" just as it will be proper to say "some men are over five feet tall." The characteristic of being universal or particular is referred to as the "quantity" of a proposition.

b) DISTRIBUTION: The meaning of a standard form categorical proposition can be further explained by utilizing a technical word, namely, the word "distribution." The term distribution has to do with whether the subject and predicate terms refer to an entire class or to only part of a class. When a term is distributed, reference is being made to all members of the class designated by that term; when a term is *un*distributed, reference is being made to only a part of the members of the class designated by that term. The general principle controlling distribution is that a universal proposition distributes its subject term and a negative proposition distributes its predicate term.

1. AN "A" PROPOSITION: This kind of proposition has its subject distributed and its predicate undistributed. In the proposition "all dogs are animals," something is said about each and every dog, namely, that it is an animal. What is said about each and every animal? The answer is nothing; we only know that the dog class occupies a part of the animal class. There is nothing that the proposition tells us about every animal, hence the predicate term is undistributed. A singular "A" proposition has the same distribution since in "Mary is a flirt" we are including "the whole of Mary" in the flirt class.

2. AN "E" PROPOSITION: This kind of proposition distributes both its subject and predicate terms. For the proposition "no dogs are cats," we are told that each and every dog is excluded from the cat class and that each and every cat is excluded from the class of dogs. A singular "E" proposition has the same distribution since when we say "Mary is not a flirt," we are excluding "the whole of Mary" from the whole class of flirts.

3. AN "I" PROPOSITION: This kind of proposition distributes neither its subject nor predicate. The proposition "some dogs are collies" tells us nothing about every dog nor do we, on the basis of this proposition, know anything about every collie. It is true that we do know something about every collie, namely, that each and every collie is a dog, but this information is not given by the sentence at hand. To interpret the proposition as only telling us something about some collies may sound strange because we think that this implies that some collies are not dogs. However, according to our definition of "some" it does not imply this—"some" means at least one and this leaves open the possibility of "all." If you examine three students in a class and find them wearing clothes, you are entitled to say "some students in the class are wearing clothes." You certainly would not infer from this that some students are not wearing clothes.

4. AN "O" PROPOSITION: This type of proposition has its sub-

ject undistributed and its predicate distributed. The proposition "some dogs are not collies" is obviously only telling us about part of the dog class. But what is perhaps not so obvious, it is telling us something about the entire collie class—it is saying that each and every collie is excluded from the group of dogs referred to by the subject term.

c) SUMMARY: The reason for there being only four kinds of standard form propositions can be seen from the following two considerations: First, from the point of view of the categories of affirmative-negative and universal-particular, there are only four possible combinations: universal-affirmative; universal-negative; particular-affirmative; particular-negative. Second, there are only four possibilities of distribution: subject and not predicate; subject and predicate; neither subject nor predicate; not subject but predicate. Using D for distributed and U for undistributed this material can be summarized in the following table:

"A"	universal-affirmative	All	D	are	U
"E"	universal-negative	No	D	are	D
"I"	particular-affirmative	Some	U	are	U
"O"	particular-negative	Some	U	are not	D
"A"	singular-affirmative		D	is	U
"E"	singular-negative		D	is not	D

3. The logical form of a categorical syllogism

Before stating the rules of validity for the categorical syllogism the basis upon which these rules rest must be made clear. Underlying the rules is the notion of logical form: a valid syllogism is valid because of its form alone.

a) MEANING OF LOGICAL FORM: Logical form is concerned with the relation between the different terms of the argument rather than with the particular terms an argument might happen to have. When the terms of the premises are related in a proper form they will always result in propositions which will necessarily imply a conclusion. The rules governing the use of "all," "no," and "some" are such that inferences based on some arrangements are valid and others invalid. The following form, for example, is one in which any number of valid and only valid arguments can be placed—it has three "A" propositions with the subject of one premise being the same as the predicate of the other premise, and with the subject of the latter premise becoming the subject of the conclusion and the predicate of the former premise becoming the predicate of the conclusion. No matter what terms the letters are allowed to stand for, if the premises are true the conclusion must be true. Any argument with this form will be valid:

All A is B
All C is A
Therefore, All C is B

b) TESTING BY VALID FORMS: There are 24 valid forms and one method of testing for validity would be to memorize the 24 valid forms and then check actual arguments against the list to see if they matched any of the forms. This method, though cumbersome, was in wide use in the Middle Ages. The 24 valid forms are arrived at by examining all 256 possible forms and observing each form to see whether it could be filled in so that the premises are true and the conclusion false. If this could be done, the form would be an invalid one. The list of 256 is the result of taking all possible combinations of premises and conclusion such as "AAA," "AEE," "EAE," etc. and also considering the position of the middle term. (The middle term is the term that appears in both premises—in the valid form above it is "A" and in the first example following it is "B.")

The following forms are examples of invalid forms in that they can be filled in so that the premises are true and the conclusion false.

All A is B ⟶ All dogs are animals
All C is B ⟶ All cats are animals
Therefore, All C is A ⟶ All cats are dogs

All A is B ⟶ All dogs are animals
No C is A ⟶ No cats are dogs
Therefore, No C is B ⟶ No cats are animals

c) TESTING BY ANALOGIES: The use of the 24 valid forms to test arguments for validity suggests another kind of test, namely, the use of illustrative analogies. The notion of logical form lies behind such analogies. If we are given an argument such as "all communists are supporters of minority groups and all liberals are supporters of minority groups, therefore all liberals are communists," we might reply by saying "why that is like claiming that because all dogs are animals and all cats are animals, therefore all cats are dogs." If two arguments have the same form but in one argument we find true premises producing a false conclusion, how do we know the same thing is not being done in the other argument? The answer is, of course, that we can't know, and this is what is meant by saying the form is an invalid one. A valid form is such that true premises will always produce a true conclusion. Though the use of illustrative analogies is very effective in debate situations, there is the practical difficulty of being able to think up an analogy for many arguments, and also, analogies are only an effective proof of invalidity.

4. Rules of validity for the categorical syllogism

A more effective and a simpler method of testing arguments for validity other than using a list of valid forms or thinking up illustrative analogies is to use a set of rules which will serve to identify valid forms and to which a valid argument must conform. An invalid argument will then be one that breaks one or more of the rules.

a) *There must be three terms each of which is used twice.* The reason for this rule is rooted in the very nature of the categorical syllogism; the conclusion relates two terms and it can do this because each term has been related to a common term—the middle term—in the premises. In the valid syllogism "all dogs are animal and all collies are dogs; therefore, all collies are animals," all collies can be included in the class of animals because the premises have related both collies and animals to a common class—dogs. The middle term has "mediated" the relationship. A violation of this rule is called a "four term fallacy." The fact that a term is plural one time and singular another time is of no logical importance. It should be noted also that if the word "dogs" in the first proposition of the argument were changed to the synonym "canines," the argument would then have four words but still only three terms—a term is what a word means.

A crude example in which this rule is broken might be "all dogs are animals, all roses are flowers, therefore all roses are animals." Perhaps nobody would be fooled by such an argument, but the following more subtle example has been accepted as a good argument by many people: "all laws have a lawmaker, nature has laws, therefore nature has a lawmaker." There are only three class words in this argument but there are four terms—the word "laws" is being used in two different senses. In the first proposition, "laws" means "commands of a government;" while in the second proposition, "laws" means "observed regularities."

b) *The middle term must be distributed at least once*. The two terms in the conclusion must have something in common or they cannot be put together in the conclusion. The middle term is what the two terms of the conclusion have in common, but this is only true when at least one of the terms in the conclusion is related to the whole of the class designated by the middle term. If the middle term is not thus distributed, each of the other two terms may refer to a different part of the class designated by the middle term and thus never be related to each other. A violation of this rule is called an "undistributed middle term." An example would be: "All beagles are animals. All collies are animals. Therefore, all collies are beagles."

c) *If a term is distributed in the conclusion it must be distributed in a premise*. A term that is distributed in the conclusion is referring to a whole class and this cannot be done if only a part of the class has been referred to in a premise. The conclusion of an argument cannot say more than is implicitly contained in the premises. It should be noted that an argument that has an "I" proposition for a conclusion could not possibly break this rule. The rule is not saying that terms distributed in the premises must be distributed in the conclusion. It is quite all right to be talking about all of a class in a premise and to go on to part of the class in the conclusion. When, however, there is an increase in distribution in going from the premises to the conclusion, the fallacy of "illicit process" is committed. An example is: "All dogs are four-legged creatures. All dogs are animals. Therefore, all animals are four-legged creatures."

d) *If both premises are affirmative, the conclusion must be affirmative.* A negative conclusion would assert that one class is excluded from another class, but this can only be justified when in the premises one of these classes has been excluded from the class designated by the middle term. A violation of this rule is called "drawing a negative conclusion from affirmative premises." An example is: "All dogs are animals. All collies are dogs. Therefore, no collies are animals."

e) *If one premise is negative, the conclusion must be negative.* An affirmative conclusion asserts that one class is contained in another class. This can be done only if the middle term is contained in one of the classes designated in the conclusion and itself contains the other class. This implies that both premises must be affirmative, *i.e.,* they must assert class inclusion. A violation of this rule is called the fallacy of "drawing an affirmative conclusion from a negative premise." An example would be: "All dogs are animals. No trees are dogs. Therefore, all trees are animals."

f) *If both premises are negative, no conclusion can necessarily be drawn.* It can very well be the case that when the two terms of the conclusion are both denied of the middle term in the premises, they could be denied or affirmed of each other in the conclusion. A violation of this rule is called "two negative premises." An example would be: "No collies are fish. No dogs are fish. Therefore, no dogs are collies."

5. Summary

After a piece of discourse has been identified as a categorical deductive argument and it is set up with the conclusion last, then, if the propositions are in standard form, the validity of the argument can be determined by a set of simple rules. The rule stating that a categorical syllogism must have only three terms should be applied first (the reason for this will become clear later), but then the other rules can be applied in any order. It is probably easiest to use rules D, E, and F next since they can be applied in one synthetic glance. This is the case since they all deal with quality and can be reduced to the single rule that "either all of the propositions must be affirmative, or one premise must be negative and the conclusion negative." The third and fourth steps would then consist in applying the rules of quantity that deal with the distribution of the middle term and the distribution of terms in the conclusion.

EXERCISE #3:
STANDARD FORM CATEGORICAL PROPOSITIONS
(For Chapter Two, sections I and II)

For the following propositions: 1) identify the subject and predicate terms; 2) state the quality and quantity of each proposition; 3) give the name (AEIO) of each proposition; 4) state the distribution for each proposition.

1. Some girls are actresses.
2. No Americans are cowards.
3. All professors are scholars.
4. Some guns are not rifles.
5. Some men who never read are profound students of nature.
6. Mary is a good girl.
7. No girls are successful weight lifters.
8. This book is a history book.
9. The first day of the week is not Tuesday.
10. All members of this class are persons who have done reasonably well on the entrance examination.
11. No persons in the United States Senate are women who do not have some college education.
12. Some books that are long, dry, and full of unimportant information are books that are very useful to people who expect to spend their lives on quiz programs.
13. John is not a football player.
14. Some stars that fall on a summer night are not members of a constellation that can be seen by the naked eye.
15. All cows that give milk which is not consumed by the farmer are animals that could yield a profit if they were properly cared for.

EXERCISE #4: CATEGORICAL SYLLOGISM
(For Chapter Two, sections III and IV)

Rewrite the following syllogisms with the conclusion last (if necessary) and indicate whether the argument is valid or invalid. If invalid, state which rule is broken.

1. Some men are not successes and no successes are lazy, therefore, some men are lazy.

2. Moby Dick is not a fish because Moby Dick is a mammal and no fish is a mammal.

3. Since some chairs are soft things, some stools are not chairs, for no stools are soft things.

4. All Russians are people who hold these opinions and John is a person who holds these opinions, so John is a Russian.

5. No cloudy days are good days for taking pictures, and no August days are cloudy days, therefore, all August days are good days for taking pictures.

6. Some harmful drinks are not cocktails because all cocktails are alcoholic drinks and all alcoholic drinks are harmful drinks.

7. Since this kettle is metal, this kettle is not a compound substance, because no metal is a compound substance.

8. All people interested in international peace are people interested in progress because all people interested in progress are good citizens and all good citizens are people interested in international peace.

9. All wealthy people are people who live in the suburbs, and all people who like to live in the suburbs are people who would dislike the dirt of the city, so all wealthy people are people who would dislike the dirt of the city.

10. Some statesmen are traitors, for all traitors are fools and some statesmen are fools.

11. Since no American is a person who likes slavery and all morons are people who like slavery, no American is a moron.

12. Because all rabbits are cowards, it follows that some cute animals are cowards, since some rabbits are not cute animals.

13. Since no turtles are speedy runners, no turtles are healthy creatures, for all fast runners are healthy creatures.

14. Since some apes are powerful creatures, no apes are sickly creatures, since no sickly creatures are powerful creatures.

15. All teachers who can't control their pupils are poor disciplinarians. All cross-eyed teachers are teachers who can't control their pupils. Therefore, all cross-eyed teachers are poor disciplinarians.

Chapter III

RELATIONS AMONG PROPOSITIONS

In the discourse of ordinary language and everyday speech, arguments of the categorical syllogistic type are not usually found with propositions in standard form. A typical example of a syllogism in everyday speech might be the following: "Since only intelligent students participate in seminars, freshmen must not be intelligent since all seminar participants are non-freshmen."

This sort of argument poses three new problems: 1) The first two propositions are not in standard form. What is the subject term of the first proposition? Is the second proposition particular or universal? What is the distribution of terms in each proposition? What is involved in the grammatical change of ordinary language into standard form propositions? 2) There are four terms in the argument, yet two of the terms—"freshmen" and "non-freshmen"—seem to be related. Can standard form propositions be logically translated so that one term can be replaced by another? What are the processes for changing a standard form proposition into an equivalent standard form proposition? 3) What is the relation between "freshmen" and "non-freshmen"? What is the total set of logical relations among propositions? The next three sections will take up these problems.

1. Logical relations among propositions

By logical relations among propositions is meant the relations of truth and falsity that hold between any two propositions. For example, if we know that the proposition "all A is B" is true, we can deduce that the proposition "no A is B" must be false—it is impossible that these two propositions be true together. A knowledge of these relations is important both for telling us what the implications of a given proposition might be, and also, for the clarification of the distinction between contradiction and contrariety. As will be seen in the next chapter, a knowledge of this distinction is vital to an evaluation of the syllogism as it functions in everyday discourse.

There are only six logical relations among propositions and any two propositions must be related to each other by one and only one of these relations. The study of these relations sometimes goes under the name of immediate inference in contrast to the mediate inference of the syllogism. Whereas in the syllogism the inference from one proposition to a conclusion is mediated by a second premise, in immediate inference the inference is made directly from one proposition to another proposition. If we know that "all A is B," we can directly deduce that "some A is B" is true and that it is false to say that "no A is B" or that "some A is not B." The six logical relations are as follows:

a) INDEPENDENCE: Two propositions are related as independent when the truth or falsity of either one has no effect on the truth or falsity of the other. For example, "all dogs are animals" and "all roses are flowers" have the relation of independence to each other. If one of the propositions is known to be true, nothing can be inferred about the truth or falsity of the other; if one of the propositions is false, again nothing can be inferred about the other. Letting "P" stand for the proposition whose value is known and "Q" for the other, this relation can be defined by a truth table as follows:

P	Q
T	?
F	?

b) EQUIVALENCE: Two propositions are related as equivalent when, of necessity, they are true together and false together. An example is "all metals are conductors" and "no metals are non-conductors." If one of the propositions is true, the other must be true, and if one is false the other must be false. Any two propositions that are related in this way are logically equivalent in meaning, even though there may be shades of difference in connotation between the propositions. Again, a truth table will define this relation:

P	Q
T	T
F	F

c) CONTRADICTION: Two propositions are contradictory when if one is true the other is false, and if one is false the other is true. Two contradictory propositions cannot both be true nor can they both be false. An "A" proposition and an "O" proposition with the same subject and predicate, or an "E" proposition and an "I" proposition with the same subject and predicate fall into this category: for example, "all crows are black" and "some crows are not black." Applying the definition of contradiction to singular "A" and "E" propositions with the same subject and predicate reveals that they are related as contradictories: for example, "John is white" and "John is not white." A truth table definition would be:

P	Q
T	F
F	T

d) CONTRARIETY: Two propositions are related as contraries when if one is true the other is false but if one is false the other is undetermined. It is impossible for two contrary propositions to both be true though they both may be false. At least one of a pair of contrary propositions must be false and maybe they both are false. A general "A" proposition and a general "E" proposition with the same subject and predicate are related as contraries. An example is "all girls are pretty" and "no girls are pretty." If one of these propositions is true then the other must be false, but if one is false then the other is undetermined. The same relationship holds between two singular "A" propositions such as "John is black" and "John is white." If one is true the other is false; but if, for example, "John is black" is false, it can not be determined that "John is white" is true—John may be brown. Defined on a truth table the relation is as follows:

P	Q
T	F
F	?

e) <u>SUBCONTRARIETY</u>: This relation is the opposite of the relation of contrariety. The character of this kind of relation is that at least one of a pair of propositions is true and maybe both are true; they both can't be false. An "I" proposition and an "O" proposition with the same subject and predicate are related as subcontraries. If the proposition "some men are handsome" is true, nothing can be determined from this alone about the truth of "some men are not handsome," but if it is false that some men are handsome, then we can infer that there must be some men who are not handsome. It must be remembered that an "I" proposition such as "some men are handsome" is not saying that some and only some men are handsome—it is saying that *at least* one man is handsome and maybe all men are handsome. In like manner, an "O" proposition leaves open the possibility of an 'E' proposition being true. This being the case, it is impossible to infer from "some men are handsome" to "some men are not handsome" nor from "some men are not handsome" to "some men are handsome," but if one of these propositions is false, then we can infer that the other must be true. Two singular "E" propositions such as "John is not black" and "John is not white" are also related as subcontraries. It is clear that if one of these propositions is true it tells us nothing about the other proposition, but what takes some thought is to see that if one of the propositions is false, the other must be true. This is most readily observed by going through a chain of thought as follows: if it is false that John is not black then he must be black, and if he is black, then it is true to say he is not white. Subcontrariety is defined on a truth table as follows:

P	Q
T	?
F	T

f) <u>IMPLICATION</u>: In order to define the relation of implication two truth tables are needed. Two propositions "P" and

"Q," are related by implication if when "P" is true "Q" is true, and when "P" is false "Q" is undetermined; then if we start with "Q" we find that when "Q" is true "P" is undetermined and when "Q" is false "P" is false. An "A" and an "I" proposition with the same subject and predicate or an "E" and an "O" with the same subject and predicate are examples of this relation.

If "all girls are pretty" is true, then "some girls are pretty" is true, but if "all girls are pretty" is false, then "some girls are pretty" is undetermined. This is the case because it might be that no girls are pretty. On the other hand, if the second proposition is true we can not determine the first proposition because it might be that some girls are pretty and some girls are not pretty. However, if "some girls are pretty" is false, then we know "all girls are pretty" must be false. This relation of implication differs from the other five relations in that it is not symmetrical. For the other relations, the truth table is the same no matter which proposition is called "P," but for implication the truth table will differ. Calling the "A" proposition "P" will result in the table on the left, whereas calling the "I" proposition "P" will yield the table on the right. Sometimes a distinction is made within the relation of implication by calling the table on the left "superimplication" and the table on the right "subimplication."

P	Q		P	Q
T	T		T	?
F	?		F	F

g) SUMMARY: The logical relations can be summarized in a truth table or through a device known as the square of opposition.

1. TRUTH TABLE SUMMARY: Letting "P" and "Q" stand for any two propositions, the relation between the two propositions can be determined by seeing which of the following truth values fits the case. Though the bottom two lines of the table are the same as the top two for the first five relations and hence unnecessary, the relation of implication demands the four line truth table.

	Ind.	Equ.	Contrd.	Cont.	Subco.	Imp.
If P is T, then Q is	?	T	F	F	?	T
If P is F, then Q is	?	F	T	?	T	?
If Q is T, then P is	?	T	F	F	?	?
If Q is F, then P is	?	F	T	?	T	F

2. THE SQUARE OF OPPOSITION: A square of opposition is an interesting memory device that can be used to determine four of the six relations but only for standard form propositions (not including singular propositions) with the same subject and predicate.

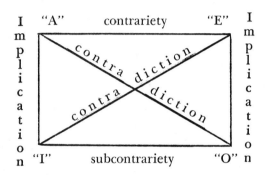

2. Logical translations of equivalences

By logical translations of equivalences is meant the process whereby a standard form proposition is changed into another standard form proposition with the same meaning. An example would be the change of "all men are mortal" to "no men are immortal." This process is called a logical translation because it proceeds by regular rules and is therefore in contrast to the rather intuitive procedures involved in the grammatical translations discussed in the next section. The two propositions are said to be "logically equivalent" because the equivalence is established by an inspection of the form of the propositions.

Logical translation is not only useful in its own right as a way of determining whether different sentences are saying the same thing, but also, it is vital to the evaluation of syllogisms that appear to have more than three terms but actually only have three terms. The following syllogism is a case in point:

"All metals are conductors and all icons are non-conductors, hence no icons are metals." By changing either the first proposition to "no metals are non-conductors" or the second proposition to "no icons are conductors," the number of terms can be reduced to three and the argument properly evaluated.

a) OBVERSION: To translate a standard form proposition into an equivalent standard form proposition by the process of obversion is to change the quality of the proposition (not the quantity) and to change the predicate to its contradictory, *i.e.*, to a term that refers to all objects other than those referred to by the predicate term. An example would be changing "all metals are conductors" to "no metals are non-conductors." The principle behind this process is the familiar one of two negatives making a positive. When a word like "mortal" has an established contradictory like "immortal," it is correct and natural to use this contradictory; however, care must be taken not to use a contrary instead of a contradictory term. To obvert "all men are brave" to "no men are cowards" is not correct. To call all men brave is to exclude them from the class of cowards, but also it is to exclude them from the class of most people who are neither brave nor cowardly. To say no men are cowards is to allow them to be in the class of most people. A safe though awkward procedure is to form the contradictory of the predicate by using the prefix "non." Following this method, the obverse of "all men are brave" would be "no men are non-brave." In similar vein, if a statement has a clause in the predicate, it should be obverted by using the word "not." Thus, "all students are persons in the front row" becomes "no students are persons not in the front row." The following table indicates the obverse of each kind of standard form proposition:

"All metals are conductors" to "No metals are non-conductors."

"No commuters are residents" to "All commuters are non-residents."

"Some students are freshmen" to "Some students are not non-freshmen."

"Some men are not Americans" to "Some men are non-Americans."

"Joe is a player" to "Joe is not a non-player."
"Mary is not a student" to "Mary is a non-student."

b) CONVERSION: A second process of logical translation into
equivalence is conversion. To convert a standard form proposition, the order of the subject and the predicate must be
changed. For example, "no dogs are cats" converts into the
equivalent proposition "no cats are dogs," and "some girls are
flirts" converts into "some flirts are girls." Since to change the
order of an "A" or an "O" proposition will result in increasing
the distribution of one of the terms and thus changing the
meaning of the proposition, such propositions cannot be simply converted. An "O" proposition can never be converted but
an "A" proposition can be converted in three exceptional
ways:

1) An "A" proposition can always be converted by reducing
the proposition to an "I" proposition. Thus, "all dogs are
animals" converts to "some animals are dogs." It should be
observed that by changing the quantity, the result of this
conversion by limitation is not, strictly speaking, an equivalent
proposition. 2) A definition can be converted because the subject and predicate apply to the same objects. To say a triangle
is a three-sided plane figure is to say all three-sided plane
figures are triangles. This sort of conversion requires special
knowledge of the subject matter dealt with by the original
proposition. 3) A definite description such as "John is the
tallest person in his class" can be converted to "The tallest
person in his class is John." In this situation, the word "is" is
not the "is" of predication but is the "is" of identity. The
description is one that applies only to the subject, hence it
makes no logical difference which term comes first. The word
"the" in the predicate is a clear indication that a definite
description is present. Definite descriptions, as well as the
definitions mentioned above, are not "A" propositions as we
have defined them, but rather, are statements that look like "A"
propositions.

c) CONTRAPOSITION: To form the contrapositive of a proposition the order of the subject and predicate must be changed
and then each term contradicted. This process is not only a
restricted one in that it only applies to "A" and "O" proposi-

tions, but it also is a derivative process. If a person questions the equivalence of "no dogs are cats" to "no cats are dogs," there is nothing much to be said, but if a person questions the equivalence of "all collies are dogs" to "all non-dogs are non-collies," the equivalence can be shown by going through a series of obversions and conversions. The fact that a series such as the following would be stopped after the second step for "E" and "I" propositions indicates why these propositions have no contrapositive (an "E" proposition has a contrapositive by limitation).

"all collies are dogs"
"no collies are non-dogs"   obverse of first proposition
"no non-dogs are collies"   converse of second proposition
"all non-dogs are non-collies"   obverse of third proposition—
                                   is called the contrapositive of
                                   the first proposition.

3. Grammatical translations

Before the rules of validity can be applied to a syllogism the propositions must be in standard form so that the relation between the classes is clearly indicated. It is obviously impossible to judge the validity of an argument when the meaning of the propositions in the argument is not understood. There are certain typical situations for which translation rules can be learned, but many cases can only be determined by sensitivity to language usage. It is this latter situation that distinguishes what we are calling "grammatical translation" from the mechanical procedures of the "logical translations" of the preceding section. The basic question to be asked of any translation into standard form is: "does the translation have the same meaning as the original proposition?" The relation between the standard form proposition and the original proposition must be one of equivalence, *i.e.,* if one proposition is true, the other must be true and if one is false, the other must be false.

a) THE SUBJECT NOT FIRST IN A PROPOSITION: The most important task is to determine the subject of a proposition. If a proposition sounds affirmative and universal, the subject will be distributed and the predicate will not be distributed, hence, it is vital that the subject be identified. For example, in "Into the night rode Lochinvar," the subject is "Lochinvar." A standard form translation might be "Lochinvar is a person who rode into the night." Another common situation occurs when a clause is part of the subject but is separated from it by other words. The sentence "all played who practiced" has the clause "who practiced" separated from the word "all" which it modifies. The standard form version of the proposition would be "all persons who practiced are persons who played."

b) THE LACK OF A CLASS TERM FOR A PREDICATE: Instead of a term that refers to a class of objects such as "books," "boys in the first row," etc., the predicate may only be an adjective such as "red," "fast," etc. It may seem pedantic to insist upon changing "all lions are fierce" to "all lions are fierce creatures," but unless this is done, careless mistakes are likely to occur. For example, the following may mistakenly be called a four term fallacy: "All lions are fierce and all fierce creatures are meat-eaters, therefore, all lions are meat-eaters."

c) THE ABSENCE OF A COPULA: Frequently in everyday discourse verbs other than the present tense of the verb "to be" are used. Sentences such as "some birds sing" are changed into standard form by changing the verb "sing" (with any attending characteristics such as "loudly," etc.) into the class predicate term "singers" or "creatures that sing" and inserting the copula "are" between the subject and predicate. The resulting translation is "some birds are singers." A variant of this situation is where a tense other than the present tense of the verb "to be" is used. If a sentence occurs such as "John was a Texan," it should be changed to "John is a person who was a Texan." This sounds awkward but it will prevent mistakes like calling the following argument valid: "All Texans are Americans and John was a Texan, hence John is an American."

d) ABSENCE OF A QUANTIFIER: In the proposition "children are cruel," sometimes what is meant is that some children are cruel but most frequently the intention is universal. An indication of this is that in the argument "children are cruel and John is a child, hence John is cruel," the normal response would be "not all children are cruel." The fact that this response would be made indicates that we understood the argument to be claiming that all children are cruel. A safe rule to use in dealing with propositions without quantifiers is that they are to be treated as universals unless there is no doubt but that the intention is particular. For example, the proposition "humans live to age one hundred" has an obvious particular intention.

e) THE USE OF NON-STANDARD QUANTIFIERS: Many times instead of the words "all," "no," or "some," words like "every," "any," "none," "one," "a few," "many," "most," etc. will be used. The translation of such terms is as follows: "every," and "any" become "all;" "none" becomes "no;" "one," "a few," "many," "most," become "some." The words "a" and "an" sometimes refer to all and sometimes to some; a sensitivity to intention is the only safeguard here. The sentence "a fly is an insect" is clearly universal whereas "a fly is in the room" is just as clearly particular.

f) DENIAL OF A UNIVERSAL AFFIRMATIVE PROPOSITION: Superficially, propositions such as "not all girls are flirts" or "all girls are not flirts" look like "E" propositions. However, when attention is paid to the meaning of the propositions it is evident that what is meant is the "O" proposition "some girls are not flirts." The normal context of such statements is after a person has asserted that "all girls are flirts." The intention is to deny this statement and the denial is formulated as "not all girls are flirts." Since it only takes one girl who is not a flirt to deny the original statement, the denial must mean "some girls are not flirts." The square of opposition makes this clear when it shows that the contradiction of an "A" proposition is an "O" proposition.

g) EXCLUSIVE PROPOSITIONS: Another common usage is found in propositions such as "only students are candidates," or "none but students are candidates," or "students alone are candidates." These propositions are called exclusive propositions because they are saying that the predicate ("candidates") applies exclusively to the subject ("students"). Exclusive propositions can be put into standard form by dropping the "only," "none but," or "alone," making the predicate of the exclusive proposition the subject and the subject the predicate, and using "all" for the quantifier. It is useful to keep a clear case in mind such as "only females are mothers" which changes into "all mothers are females."

h) <u>EXCEPTIVE PROPOSITIONS</u>: Sometimes the words "only," "none but," and "alone" function in an exceptive sense. An exceptive proposition is one that is normally understood to be making two assertions rather than one. An example would be "only the president can attend the meeting." This sentence is saying that "all who can attend the meeting is the president," but it also seems to be saying that "the president is a person who can attend the meeting." The more frequent and explicit kind of exceptive sentence is where the word "except" (or "save" or "but") itself is used. The sentence "all except officers are admitted" translates into the two sentences "all persons admitted are non-officers" and "all non-officers are persons admitted." The same situation holds for certain numerical sentences that begin with "almost all," "all but a few," "few," etc. The sentence "almost all of the students are at the dance" is saying "some students are at the dance" but it is also denying that all students are at the dance. This denial would be stated as "some students are not at the dance."

i) <u>PROPOSITIONS NEEDING PARAMETERS</u>: A sentence such as "we get cold whenever we are outside in below-zero weather" clearly intends an "A" proposition with the second part as the subject. The difficulty begins when an attempt is made to word the proposition in standard form. A solution is to use a parameter or helping word such as "times" and then the sentence can be worded as "all times when we are outside in below-zero weather are times when we get cold." Other useful parameters are "places" and "occasions."

j) <u>SUMMARY TABLE OF COMMON GRAMMATICAL TRANSLATIONS</u>:

1. Little is done by fools. All fools are people who do little.
2. All teachers are kind. All teachers are kind persons.
3. All frogs leap. All frogs are leaping creatures.
4. Cats are cowards. All cats are cowards.
5. Many men are voters. Some men are voters.
6. Not all Germans are Nazis. Some Germans are not Nazis.
7. Only men are philosophers. All philosophers are men.

8. All except babies are doers. All non-babies are doers.
   All doers are non-babies.

9. He coughs whenever he smokes. All times when he smokes are times when he coughs.

EXERCISE #5: LOGICAL RELATIONS
(For Chapter Three, section I)

a) State the relationship between the following pairs of propositions:

1. All rabbits are cowards.
   Some rabbits are not cowards.

2. Some rabbits are not cowards.
   Some rabbits are cowards.

3. Some rabbits are cowards.
   No rabbits are cowards.

4. No rabbits are cowards.
   All rabbits are vegetarians.

5. All rabbits are vegetarians.
   No rabbits are vegetarians.

6. No rabbits are vegetarians.
   Some rabbits are not vegetarians.

7. Some rabbits are not vegetarians.
   Some rabbits are vegetarians.

8. The book is red.
   The book is black.

9. The book is not red.
   The book is not black.

10. The book is red.
    The book is not red.

11. The word "the" is the first word in the Bible.
    The word "God" is the first word in the Bible.

12. The word "the" is not the first word in the Bible.
    The word "God" is not the first word in the Bible.

13. Napoleon was militaristic.
    Napoleon was not militaristic.

14. Some children are not kind.
    Some children are kind.

15. All men are mortal.
    No men are immortal.

b) If the first proposition in each of the following groups is true, what can be inferred about the truth or falsity of the other propositions in the group?

1. (a) All girls are flirts.
   (b) No girls are flirts.
   (c) Some girls are flirts.
   (d) Some girls are not flirts.

2. (a) No men are mortal.
   (b) All men are mortal.
   (c) Some men are mortal.
   (d) Some men are not mortal.

3. (a) Some men are not scholars.
   (b) Some men are scholars.
   (c) All men are scholars.
   (d) No men are scholars.

4. (a) Some A is B.
   (b) Some A is not B.
   (c) All A is B.
   (d) No A is B.

5. (a) This book is red all over.
   (b) This book is not red all over.
   (c) This book is blue all over.
   (d) This book is not blue all over.

c) If the first proposition in each of the above groups is false, what can be inferred about the truth or falsity of the other propositions in the group?

EXERCISE #6: LOGICAL EQUIVALENCES
(For Chapter Three, section II)

a) State the obverse of the following propositions:

1. No men are angels.
2. Some dogs are hunters.

3. All men are mortal.

4. Some birds are not singers.

5. John is a coward.

6. She is not a good cook.

7. All of the players are students who had not gone to the dance.

8. Some of the people in the first row are not persons who have tickets.

9. No animals that have fur are creatures that fear the cold.

10. Some American statesmen are men who do not carry important papers.

11. Some Russian statesmen are not men who carry important papers.

12. This book is not a best seller.

b) State the converse of the following propositions:

1. No children are parents.

2. All metals are conductors.

3. Some trees are not oaks.

4. Some men are cowards.

5. No person in America is a person with two heads.

6. Some people who studied hard are people who will get good grades.

7. Washington is the first president of the United States.

8. Some animals that build nests are not songbirds.

9. All squares are figures with four equal sides.

10. No member of the United Nations is a nation that is defined as being war-like.

c) State the contrapositive of the following propositions:

1. No girls are mailmen.

2. Some girls are conductors.

3. Some dogs are not collies.

4. All voters are residents.

5. All students who live in dormitories are persons eligible to vote in the student election.

d) If the proposition "all girls are flirts" is true, what can be inferred about the truth or falsity of the following propositions?

1. All flirts are girls.
2. Some girls are flirts.
3. All non-flirts are non-girls.
4. No girls are non-flirts.
5. Some flirts are girls.
6. No flirts are non-girls.
7. All non-girls are non-flirts.
8. Some flirts are not non-girls.
9. Some girls are not non-flirts.
10. Some non-girls are not flirts.
11. Some girls are not flirts.
12. Some flirts are not girls.

EXERCISE #7: ORDINARY LANGUAGE
(For Chapter Three, section III)

Translate each of the following sentences into a standard form categorical proposition with an equivalent meaning:

1. Little is taught by ignorant people.
2. Mary is not tall.
3. Everyone received an "A" who did the work.
4. Not all of the students are in a fraternity.
5. Few students are grandmothers.
6. Dogs are friendly.
7. Senators alone can vote in the Senate.
8. Dogs live to the age of fifteen.
9. Many persons are allergic to smoke.
10. Only citizens can vote.
11. All of the dogs in town are not dirty.
12. A few students are tardy.
13. None but artists are qualified to judge works of art.

14. To know her is to love her.
15. Only the president can pardon a prisoner.
16. A banana is a fruit.
17. He laughs best who laughs last.
18. What goes in one end must come out the other end.
19. Nothing is both good in theory and bad in practice.
20. All that glitters is not gold.
21. A bird sits on the fence.
22. If a book is interesting, then it will be read.
23. Almost all of the members went to the dance.
24. Everyone except the entertainers went to the reception.
25. All of the people laughed whenever a joke was told.

Chapter IV

THE CATEGORICAL SYLLOGISM: IRREGULAR FORMS

Whenever a categorical syllogism is in standard form the task of evaluation is the relatively simple one of applying the rules of validity. However, in everyday usage, the syllogism is frequently not in standard form and then the difficult preliminary assignment arises of placing the syllogism into standard form. There are four ways in which a deviation from standard form can occur; a syllogism may deviate in only one of these ways or it may be irregular in all four ways at one time. 1) The propositions may not be in standard form. 2) There may be apparently, though not really, four or more terms. 3) There may be only one premise and a conclusion or two premises and no conclusion. 4) A series of syllogisms may be connected together with some of the intermediate conclusions not stated. These irregularities will be taken up in order in the present chapter and then a final section will consider the syllogism as it functions in the actual context of daily life.

1. Propositions not in standard form

An example of a categorical syllogism in which the propositions are not in standard form is: "None but boys jumped because all jumped who saw the danger and only boys saw it." It is wise, particularly in the early stages of learning a new process to follow an orderly series of steps in making an analysis. The following three steps are suggested as a way of preventing hasty work and foolish mistakes:

1. Rewrite the argument with the conclusion last. Since the word "because" precedes premises, the result will then be:

All jumped who saw the danger.
Only boys saw it.
Therefore, none but boys jumped.

2. Translate each sentence that is not in standard form into standard form. Refer back to section III of chapter three for help if necessary, but remember the basic rule that the translation must have the same meaning as the original sentence.

All persons who saw the danger are persons who jumped.
All persons who saw the danger are boys.
Therefore, all persons who jumped are boys.

3. Evaluate the argument by applying the rules of validity. In this case, the argument is invalid because the subject term of the conclusion is distributed but the term is not distributed in a premise, hence there is an illicit process.

2. Apparent four term arguments

Though a categorical syllogism is invalid if it has more than three terms, the error is customarily referred to as a four term fallacy whether there are four, five, or six terms in the argument. Following this procedure, an argument might *seem* to have four, five, or six terms, but all of these cases are called apparent four term arguments. Before taking up each of these situations in turn, it is well to keep in mind that not all four term arguments are only apparently four term arguments; some four term arguments are really four term arguments. The crucial question is: "are two of the terms contradictories?" If they are, then they can be reduced to one term; but if they are not, then the argument is a four term fallacy and no amount of manipulation can remedy the error. If an argument has four terms and they can be reduced to three, this should be done first and then the rules of validity applied.

a) APPARENTLY FOUR TERMS: An example of such an argument would be "no men are immortal and Socrates is a man, hence Socrates is mortal." Since the sentences are in standard form and the conclusion is last, there is no need to do any rewriting before applying the rules of validity. Upon using the first rule, *i.e.*, an argument must have only three terms, it is seen that this argument has four terms. Further observation reveals that "mortal" and "immortal" are contradictories, hence the four terms can be reduced to three terms. This can be done by either obverting the first premise to "all men are mortal" or obverting the conclusion to "Socrates is not immortal." One way is as good as another way, though it is probably esthetically more satisfying to eliminate terms with a prefix if that is possible. After this reduction the other rules of validity must be applied and the argument then turns out to be valid.

b) APPARENTLY FIVE TERMS: A five term argument might be "all non-conductors are non-metals and some alloys are conductors, hence, some metals are alloys." Two methods of handling this argument are: 1) Obvert the second premise to "some alloys are not non-conductors;" convert the conclusion to "some alloys are metals" and then obvert this to "some alloys are not non-metals." Though conversion does not result in the change of any term except in its position, it is a necessary step if the term that demands changing in quality happens to be in the subject position. 2) Take the contrapositive of the first proposition which will change two terms in one operation and result in "all metals are conductors." When the other rules are applied to this syllogism it turns out to be invalid due to an illicit process if the first method is used and due to an undistributed middle term if the second method is used. If an argument turns out to be invalid when one method is used, there is no need to try another method in the hope that the argument will prove to be valid. Since it is the same argument, it will still show itself to be invalid though perhaps for a different reason as in the above example.

c) APPARENTLY SIX TERMS: This kind of argument would be rather rare in ordinary speech, yet something like the following might be encountered: "since no non-members are subscribers, all non-aliens are members, for all non-subscribers are aliens." In this case, though the propositions are all in standard form, the conclusion is not last, so the argument should be rewritten as follows:

No non-members are subscribers.
All non-subscribers are aliens.
Therefore, all non-aliens are members.

There are six terms consisting of three pairs of contradictory terms, hence there can be a reduction to three terms. Three ways of doing this might be: 1) Contrapose the second premise to "all non-aliens are subscribers" and obvert the conclusion to "no non-aliens are non-members." 2) Contrapose the conclusion to "all non-members are aliens" and obvert the first premise to "all non-members are non subscribers." 3) Obvert all three propositions. Since the argument proves to be valid by one method we know it will prove to be valid by any method; hence, there is no need to try more than one method.

3. The enthymeme

An enthymeme is a syllogism in which one of the premises or the conclusion is understood but not stated. An example would be "Mary can vote because she is a citizen." This form of argument is so frequently encountered in persuasive speeches that it was given the name "Rhetorical Syllogism" by Aristotle. Public speakers have found that if a syllogism has an obviously false proposition, it is good strategy to omit that proposition. The listener will mentally fill it in, but in so doing he is apt to slide over it and not notice its falsity. The critical procedure is to fill in the omitted proposition and then apply the rules of validity. The only new difficulty presented by the enthymeme is that involved in choosing the proposition to be added. For the most part these arguments are so simple that it would be rare to find a person arguing invalidly; hence, the proper procedure is to add a proposition that will make the argument valid if this is possible. In the enthymeme cited above, it is intuitively clear as well as necessary to the validity of the argument that the added proposition be the false one "all citizens can vote" instead of the true one "all persons who can vote are citizens." On the other hand, in the enthymeme "all men are mortal, hence Rex is not mortal," it is impossible to fill in a premise that will remove the illicit process and make the argument valid.

a) ENTHYMEME WITH A PREMISE OMITTED: Both of the enthymemes used in the above paragraph are examples of an enthymeme with a premise omitted. Though the omitted premise can usually be detected intuitively, yet there are mechanical aids to facilitate its discovery. If the conclusion of our enthymeme is "Mary can vote," each premise will have one of these terms plus the term that is the middle term. Thus, since the given premise has "Mary" and "citizen," the omitted premise will have "vote" and "citizen." If we know that a syllogism has three terms each of which is used twice, and that one term appears in both premises, then it should be simple to figure out which terms must be in the missing premise.

b) ENTHYMEME WITH THE CONCLUSION OMITTED: Frequently the conclusion of an argument is so obvious that it would seem pedantic for it to be stated. Suppose that in a conversation you are asked who will win the pennant in the American League. You might reply, "the team with the heaviest hitters will win and the Yankees have the heaviest hitters." There is no need to add the obvious conclusion "therefore, the Yankees will win." Since the first step in evaluating an argument is to write down the conclusion, in this kind of argument the first step is to figure out what the conclusion is and then write it down. After this is done, the usual procedure follows, namely, get the sentences into standard form if this is necessary and then apply the rules of validity.

c) ENTHYMEMES AND CAUSAL ASSERTIONS: At this point, some attention should be given to causal assertions since there is a tendency to confuse them with enthymemes. If what would be taken as the conclusion of an enthymeme is a fact known by sense experience, and if the word "because" is the logical connective, then the piece of discourse is a causal assertion. The contrast is between the argument "Mary can vote because she is a citizen," and the assertion "my head aches because I studied too hard." In the first case evidence is being presented for a conclusion whereas the second case is presenting an explanation for an obvious fact. If it is asked how we know that Mary can vote, it is reasonable to respond with "she is a citizen," but when we ask how we know my head aches, it does not make much sense to reply "I studied too hard."

4. Sorites

Another deviation from the standard form categorical syllogism is the sorites. A sorites is a chain of categorical syllogisms with only the premises and the final conclusion stated. An example with three premises (there can be any number) is as follows: "some educated persons are beautiful women because all teachers are educated persons, all blondes are beautiful women, and some teachers are blondes." The steps in testing a sorites are:

1. List the premises and the conclusion in a chain so that each proposition has a term in common with the proposition preceding it. If this cannot be done, this usually indicates that the sorites is invalid because one of the syllogisms may have four terms. It might, however, be the case that the sorites is enthymemic and a proposition can be supplied that will make a chain. In our example, if the proposition "all teachers are educated persons," had not been stated, it would be reasonable to add it and make a sorites. Taking the argument as it stands, though a chain could be made in various ways, one method would be:

All blondes are beautiful women.
Some teachers are blondes.
All teachers are educated persons.
Therefore, some educated persons are beautiful women.

2. Fill in the missing conclusions. When there are three premises there will be one missing conclusion and when there are four premises there will be two missing conclusions, and so forth. In this case, there is one missing conclusion and it will be the conclusion that follows from the first two premises: "some teachers are beautiful women."

3. Test each syllogism in the chain. When the missing conclusion is added, there will be two syllogisms: the first one will have the first two premises and the added conclusion and the second one will use the added conclusion as its first premise. If either of the syllogisms is invalid the whole sorites is invalid —a chain is only as strong as its weakest link. The principle behind the whole procedure is that any proposition implied by the premises is really a part of the argument and it can be made explicit and used. The final result would then be:

All blondes are beautiful women.
Some teachers are blondes.

Therefore, some teachers are beautiful women.
   All teachers are educated persons.

   Therefore, some educated persons are
   beautiful women.

5. Contextual arguments

By a contextual argument is meant an argument as it occurs
in newspapers, books, periodicals, speeches, etc. rather than
as it is presented in the artificial models of a logic text. The
chief problem that arises from such arguments is that of
disengaging them from the welter of logically irrelevant language and letting their "bare bones" show forth for logical
analysis. The procedure in this section will be to present a
contextual argument and then undertake one possible analysis.
It is impossible to reduce the analysis of contextual arguments to a mechanical set of rules or to one model; rather, it is
important to gain a "feel" for procedure by working with
many examples.

a) SAMPLE CONTEXTUAL ARGUMENT: This piece of discourse
was written as an editorial in the *Chicago Tribune* of March
7, 1959:

> The appointment of Sen. Stuart Symington (D., Mo.) to
> head a subcommittee for the investigation of "wasteful
> rivalry and duplication" in the space program is not likely
> to put very many people at ease.
> Not that the space program is free of suspicion. A program
> in which the three services raced against one another, with
> no coordination, was sure to result in a good deal of dupli-
> cation, and Majority Leader Johnson probably has some
> basis for saying that at least 14 agencies are involved in the
> space program today. The elimination of waste in this field
> is of the utmost importance because our national safety is
> at stake and because each instance of duplication or error
> can run into fantastic sums of money. If we are paying for
> more fireworks at Cape Canaveral than are necessary, we
> should know it.
> But Sen. Symington is no more qualified to conduct the
> proper sort of investigation than a cat is qualified to investi-

gate the construction of a robin's nest. For one thing, he has already launched his campaign for the Presidency with the charge that the Republicans have bungled the space program and that the Russians are ahead of us by four to one. His mind, quite obviously, is not open.

For another thing, there is a very delicate line between cutting out duplication and eliminating the creative rivalry which is helpful. To draw this distinction requires a good deal more technical experience in rocketry and electronics than Mr. Symington has had, even though he once headed a radio company.

Finally, Mr. Symington himself must accept some responsibility for Russia's early lead in missiles, because he was secretary of the air force during the years 1947 to 1950, when the missile program was being launched.

For these reasons we shall listen skeptically to the oratory which will doubtless flow from Sen. Symington in his new assignment. At the same time we hope that, should he happen to find any legitimate means of saving money or of increasing efficiency, those concerned will have the good sense and courage to admit it and act accordingly.

b) SAMPLE ANALYSIS: As is usual in contextual arguments, there are a number of sorites and they are complicated by the fact that they are enthymemic sorites and hence cannot be placed in a chain until all of the implicit assumptions are made explicit. It may seem foolish to elaborate a piece of discourse as we have done below, especially since all of the arguments are valid, but unless this is done there is the risk of allowing questionable assumptions to slide by unnoticed. The results of the following analysis are: first, there are two independent arguments to prove duplication in the space program; second, the conclusion of the second argument is used to prove waste in the space program; third, there are two independent arguments to prove that it is important to eliminate waste in the space program; fourth, there are three independent sorites to prove Symington is unqualified to investigate the space program. Do you accept all of the premises in the arguments below?

1. All cases where the three services race against each other with no coördination are cases that are sure to result in much duplication.

The space program is a case where the three. . . .

The space program is a case that is sure to. . . .

2. All situations where there are at least 14 agencies involved are situations of much duplication.

The space program is a situation where there are. . . .

The space program is a situation of much duplication.

3. *Ditto*

All situations of much duplication are cases of waste.

The space program is a case of waste.

4. All cases where national safety is involved are cases where elimination of waste is important.

The space program is a case where national safety is involved.

The space program is a case where elimination. . . .

5. All cases involving vast sums of money are cases where elimination of waste is important.

The space program is a case involving vast sums of money.

The space program is a case where elimination. . . .

6. No person who has announced that the Republicans have let the Russians get ahead of us is a person with an open mind.

Symington is a person who has announced. . . .

Symington is not a person with an open mind.

7. *Ditto*.

All persons qualified to conduct an investigation of the space program are persons with an open mind.

Symington is not a person qualified to conduct. . . .

8. All persons able to draw a distinction between duplication and creative rivalry are persons with experience.

Symington is not a person with experience.

Symington is not a person able to draw a distinction. . . .

9. *Ditto*

All persons qualified to conduct an investigation. . . .

Symington is not a person qualified to conduct. . . .

10. All persons who are secretaries of the air force when another country gets a lead in missiles are persons responsible for that lead.

Symington is a person who was secretary of the. . . .

Symington is a person responsible for that lead.

11. *Ditto.*

No person responsible for that lead is a person qualified to conduct. . . .

Symington is not a person qualified to conduct. . . .

EXERCISE #8: ORDINARY LANGUAGE SYLLOGISMS
(For Chapter Four, section I)

Rewrite the following arguments in standard form (if necessary) and indicate whether each argument is valid or invalid. If invalid, state which rule has been broken.

1. Since some politicians are dope-fiends, it follows that some dope-fiends are not crooks, for politicians are not all crooks.

2. Little can be done for those who may fail, because little can be done for those who do not study, and all run a chance of failing who do not study.

3. There must be a strike at the factory; for there is a picket line there, and pickets are only present at strikes.

4. Suzy must like steaks because students eat steaks and Suzy is a student.

5. Everyone is flunking who is not studying; hence John must not be studying because he is flunking.

6. All athletes are not dumb, for no dumb person graduates and many athletes do graduate.

7. Bob is eligible because none but students are eligible and Bob is a student.

8. Because intense heat is nothing else but a particular kind of pain, and pain cannot exist but in a perceiving being, it follows that no intense heat can exist in an unperceiving being.

9. Because all bums are not poor and some of the poor are unfit, it follows that some of the unfit are not bums.

10. Some students did not see the lion because everyone ran who saw the lion, but all of the students did not run.

11. It seems that the existence of God cannot be demonstrated. For it is an article of faith that God exists and what is of faith cannot be demonstrated.

12. The hounds bay wherever a fox has passed; so the fox must have taken another path, since the hounds are quiet.

13. All things immediately perceived are real things and all things immediately perceived are ideas in a mind; therefore, all real things are ideas in a mind.

14. Only boys can smoke on the campus, but since Sandy is a boy, he can smoke on the campus.

15. All except children must pay full fare. Since Joe must pay full fare, he must not be a child.

EXERCISE #9: APPARENT FOUR TERM SYLLOGISMS
(For Chapter Four, section II)

Rewrite the following arguments in standard form (if necessary) and indicate whether each argument is valid or invalid. If invalid, state which rule has been broken:

1. Since all professors are academic and business men are non-academic, it follows that no business man is a professor.

2. Since dogs are non-verbal, no dogs can be human because humans are verbal.

3. Royal College lacks school spirit, hence it needs a football team, for no college with a football team lacks school spirit.

4. Since only the brave deserve the fair and John is a coward, it follows that he does not deserve the fair.

5. Because all men are voters and all children are non-voters, it must be that some non-men are children.

6. Since all snakes are cold-blooded, no non-mammals are snakes because all cold-blooded creatures are mammals.

7. All girls are flirts because all humans are flirts and no non-humans are girls.

8. No communist is a person who believes in taking interest on money. All wealthy people have savings accounts that bear interest, hence no wealthy person is a communist.

9. No non-metal is a good conductor and all metals are costly, therefore all good conductors are costly.

10. All metals are conductors and no non-metals are malleable, hence all non-malleable things are non-conductors.

EXERCISE #10: ENTHYMEMES AND SORITES
(For Chapter Four, sections III and IV)

For the following enthymemes and sorites, supply the omitted propositions and then indicate whether the arguments are valid or invalid. If invalid, state which rule has been broken:

1. Some dogs are fierce, therefore some fierce creatures are loyal.

2. All girls are flirts and Susie is a girl.

3. Perfume smells good so this can't be perfume.

4. Umpires can do no wrong and Bill is the umpire.

5. Fascists are enemies of the human race so John is not an enemy of the human race.

6. He should succeed—he works hard.

7. Some educated people are flirts because all wrestlers are educated people, some wrestlers are women, and all women are flirts.

8. Some students are fit to sit on a committee because everyone who is fit to sit on a committee is sane, everyone who is sane can do logic, and students can do logic.

9. Since all doughnuts are round and all round things can roll, it must be true that all doughnuts are smooth since all things that can roll are smooth.

10. Since all dissatisfied creatures are unhappy, all young men are unhappy, because all idealists are sensitive creatures and all sensitive creatures are dissatisfied.

EXERCISE #11: REVIEW OF ARISTOTELIAN LOGIC
(For First Four Chapters)

For all *arguments,* either underline the conclusion or rewrite with the conclusion last and state whether the argument is valid or invalid. If invalid, state which rule is broken. If the sentences are not in standard form, the argument must be rewritten and the sentences put into standard form.

1. Judy will get a good mark because Judy is a good student.
2. Only idiots would believe that and Bob is not an idiot, so he wouldn't believe it.
3. People who study philosophy will make great accomplishments. We can see from this that great accomplishments will be made by Bob since he is studying philosophy.
4. Heavy objects fall to the ground because of the pull of gravity.
5. Soiled paper plates are scattered only where careless people have picnicked. There are soiled paper plates scattered about here. Therefore careless people must have picnicked here.
6. All who are at the game are seniors, but not all who are at the game are having a good time, so most of the seniors are not having a good time.
7. No roses can swim because all roses are creatics, all creatics are serdents, and no serdents can swim.
8. Since all combatants are courageous, no non-combatants are girls, since all courageous persons are girls.
9. All students dislike taking tests, Zeke does not take tests, therefore, Zeke is not a student.
10. All great writers are intellectuals because all great writers are eccentric and so are all intellectuals.

PART II

SYMBOLIC LOGIC

Though many deductive arguments can be handled easily by the forms of the categorical syllogism, there are many others that would stretch these forms to the breaking point. An example is: "Joe was not invited or else he was detained. If he were detained he would call the hostess. Ruth says he was invited, hence, he will call the hostess." Evaluating an argument like this by Aristotelian logic, if it is possible at all, would be analogous to doing arithmetic problems using Roman numerals. To cope with this situation modern logic has arrived at new types of inference based upon an analysis of the meaning of various compound propositions. Because of the extensive use of symbols in this new logic as well as the mechanical methods of manipulating the symbols, this logic is customarily referred to as symbolic logic. The discussion of the material in this section will proceed in three steps: first, an analysis of compound proposition forms will be made—this is basic to the entire section; second, some basic compound syllogistic forms of inference will be explained; third, all of this material with some additions, will be applied to the evaluation of irregular arguments such as the one cited above.

Chapter V

COMPOUND PROPOSITION FORMS

Before testing the validity of any argument it is necessary to know what the propositions in the argument mean. This was achieved for the categorical syllogism by placing every sentence in standard form. In like fashion, before going into the problem of the validity of arguments involving compound propositions it is necessary to establish a set of compound proposition forms with clear meanings that can be used to interpret compound propositions as they occur in ordinary language. By a compound proposition is meant an actual proposition such as "John is tall and Mary is small," whereas by a compound proposition form is meant a blank pattern to which actual propositions can conform. For example, the form of the above proposition is "P . Q" and it would be the form of the proposition even if the names were changed to Bill, Harry, Ruth, or Sam. It is customary to use letters from the end of the alphabet for proposition forms and letters from the beginning of the alphabet to symbolize propositions. Thus the compound proposition "John is tall and Mary is small" might be symbolized as "A . B" for ease of handling and this symbolization would be considered a substitution instance of the proposition form "P . Q." Our concern is with proposition forms for which any number of propositions can be viewed as substitution instances. The problem of meaning for these forms involves a new notion, namely, that meaning is determined by truth values. To ask for the difference in meaning between "John is tall and Mary is small" and "John is tall or Mary is small," is to ask how the combination of truth values of the sub-propositions affects the truth of the compound proposition. Does the first proposition claim—mean that each sub-proposition is true? That only one is true? Does the second proposition make the same claim, *i.e.,* have the same meaning as the first proposition? What determines the meanings are the connections "and" and "or," hence the problem of establishing proposition forms for compound propositions consists in defining a set of connectives, or constants, that can be used to specify the meaning of compound sentences as they occur in everyday usage.

1. The conjunctive proposition

A conjunctive proposition is one in which two sub-propositions, called conjuncts, are related by a constant called a dot (".").

a) THE CONJUNCTIVE PROPOSITION FORM: Letting "P" and "Q" stand for variables that can be filled in by any two propositions, the conjunctive proposition form will be "P . Q." What "P . Q" means is that both conjuncts are true. Since the assertion is that both conjuncts are true, the only condition under which a conjunctive proposition will be true is when both conjuncts actually are true. This definition of the dot is a truth table definition, *i.e.,* its complete meaning is specified by a table of truth values. Looking at P . Q in a truth table one can see the conditions under which it is true and the conditions under which it is false. Why is P . Q marked true on the table only when the P is true and the Q is true?—because this is what the truth claim or meaning is of the expression "P . Q." A truth table works by setting up reference columns for all of the possible combinations of truth values of P and Q and then filling in the truth value of the compound proposition by referring to the reference columns. The truth table for P . Q is:

P	Q	P . Q
T	T	T
F	T	F
T	F	F
F	F	F

b) TRANSLATION OF ORDINARY LANGUAGE: The most common connective between sub-propositions used in ordinary language that says what the dot says is the word "and;" however, there are other words such as "but," "yet," and "however" that can function in the same manner. In everyday usage, the meaning —the claim, the intention—of a proposition using one of the above connectives is that both sub-propositions are true. Thus, for the proposition "John is tall and Mary is small," we can let an "A" stand for the first sub-proposition, a "B" for the second, and connect the two symbols by a dot; this gives the proposition "A . B" the same form, *i.e.*, the same meaning as "P . Q." The fact that we can mark conjunctive propositions true or false indicates that we know what they mean, and the criterion we use in marking them true or false shows that we understand them to mean that both sub-propositions are intended to be true. If any of the following were met with on a true and false test, they would be marked true only if both sub-propositions were true:

Napoleon was German and Hitler was French.

Napoleon was French yet Hitler was French.

Napoleon was French however Hitler was German.

Zuga et bana and Tega sot lurch.

A and B.

2. The contrary disjunctive proposition

A contrary disjunctive proposition is the denial of a conjunctive proposition.

a) <u>THE SYMBOLIZATION OF DENIAL</u>: The method of denying any proposition "P" is to place a curl ("~") in front of the proposition. In ordinary language, the word "not" is used most frequently to express such a denial; thus we would deny that all girls are flirts by saying "not all girls are flirts." Another way of expressing this denial might be "it is false that all girls are flirts." It will be helpful, particularly when symbolizing long arguments, if a curl is used any time a proposition is negative in character; thus the proposition "Joe is not God" would be symbolized "~A." Also, it should be pointed out that this negative proposition is a true proposition. Just as an affirmative proposition can be false, so a negative proposition can be true. The definition of the curl on a truth table is:

P	~P
T	F
F	T

b) <u>FORM OF A CONTRARY DISJUNCTIVE PROPOSITION</u>: A contrary disjunctive proposition is formed by placing the sign of denial in front of a conjunctive proposition. At this point a problem of punctuation arises because if the sign is simply placed before the P, the result will be a conjunction that says P is false and Q is true. In order to deny the whole expression, "P . Q," it is necessary to put a parenthesis around the expression and place the curl before the parenthesis. The form of a contrary disjunctive proposition will then be: ~(P . Q). It is called "disjunctive" because the two sub-propositions are being separated, *i.e.,* "disjoined." The sub-propositions are called disjuncts. Since the meaning of a conjunction is that both sub-propositions are true, the meaning of its denial will be that they are not both true—at most one is true, at least one is false—either one is false or the other is false or both are false. As was seen in the discussion of the relations among propositions in chapter three, this is the definition of contrariety. The relation between an "A" proposition and an "E" proposition is the same as the relation that is asserted between any two propositions, P and Q, when they are related by the connective "~(.)." If the P is true, the Q must be false but if the P is false, the Q is undetermined. This must be so since "~(P . Q)" leaves open the possibility that both are false as well as the possibilities that the P is true and the Q is false or the P is false and the Q is true. The truth table definition of ~(P . Q), just the opposite of the one for conjunction, is:

P	Q	~(P . Q)
T	T	F
F	T	T
T	F	T
F	F	T

c) <u>TRANSLATION OF ORDINARY LANGUAGE</u>: The most common way of expressing a contrary disjunctive in ordinary language is through the use of the expression "not both." Thus, we might say "not both can Joe be out every night and get good grades." Other formulations might be: "Joe can't both be out every night and get good grades," or "Joe can't be out every night and at the same time get good grades." All of these expressions are claiming that two events cannot occur together, that the two sub-propositions cannot both be true. It might be that Joe stays out every night and does not get good grades, or that he does not stay out every night and gets good grades, or that he does not stay out every night and still does not get good grades, but what cannot happen, if the proposition is true, is that he stays out every night and gets good grades. The meaning of the proposition is that this cannot be the case, hence such language can be symbolized as $\sim(A . B)$ and will have the meaning of $\sim(P . Q)$.

3. The subcontrary disjunctive proposition

This type of disjunction is the converse of contrary disjunction.

a) THE FORM OF A SUBCONTRARY DISJUNCTIVE PROPOSITION: As the name indicates, the relation that is asserted between the two disjuncts is one in which at least one is true; they both can't be false—at most one is false—one is true or the other is true or both are true. The symbol used to express this relation is a wedge ("v"). The relation between "some girls are flirts" and "some girls are not flirts" is the same as that asserted for any two propositions, P and Q, when they are related by a wedge. Since they both may be true, if we know that one is true we cannot determine the other, but if we know one is false, we know the other must be true. The truth table definition of PvQ is:

P	Q	P v Q
T	T	T
F	T	T
T	F	T
F	F	F

b) TRANSLATION OF ORDINARY LANGUAGE: The English word "or" in its inclusive sense can be translated into the wedge. Supposing "Joe" to be doing well in class, someone might say "either Joe is very bright or he studies a great deal." A person making this utterance would seem to be claiming that at least one of the disjuncts must be true in order to explain Joe's success and maybe both are true. The only situation that would cause the compound proposition to be false and make the speaker a liar would be if Joe were both not bright and not a studier. This kind of proposition can be symbolized as A v B and will have the meaning of P v Q.

4. The contradictory disjunctive proposition

A contradictory disjunctive proposition is one that asserts a complete disjunction.

a) THE FORM OF A CONTRADICTORY DISJUNCTIVE PROPOSITION: The claim made by this kind of proposition is that one of the disjuncts is true and one false. To indicate this relation a wedge inside of a circle ('$\otimes$') will be used. Any two propositions, P and Q, when related by a circle-wedge, will have the same relation as "all girls are flirts" has to "some girls are not flirts." They cannot both be false nor can they both be true. If one is true, the other must be false, and if one is false the other must be true. It should be recognized that it would be possible to do without the circle-wedge and by the use of brackets state the form of a contradictory disjunction as "(P v Q) . (~P v ~Q)." This points up the fact that if propositions are extended to the point where the sub-propositions are themselves compound propositions, punctuation must be used. Without punctuation the complete proposition remains ambiguous. In arithmetic, for example, the expression "$3 \times 4 + 5$" would yield 17 when punctuated $(3 \times 4) + 5$, or 27 when punctuated $3 \times (4+5)$. Likewise, the expression "P v Q . R" has a different meaning when punctuated P v (Q . R) than it has when punctuated (P v Q) . R. In the first case, the "R" could be false and the expression as a whole be true, but in the second case the "R" must be true if the expression as a whole is true. Punctuation could be extended even further if a part of a compound sub-proposition is itself compound as in: "if Joe is either sick or hurt, and his parents are of no help, then he should get special care." This would be expressed as "[(P v Q) . R] ⊃ S." Returning to P $\otimes$ Q, its truth table definition is:

P	Q	P⊙Q
T	T	F
F	T	T
T	F	T
F	F	F

b) TRANSLATION OF ORDINARY LANGUAGE: Again the English word "or" has a use, this time the exclusive sense, that can be translated into the circle-wedge. The intention of a statement like "either Joe is in Chicago or Joe is in Paris" is that one and only one of the disjuncts is true. If Joe is in Chicago, then he cannot be in Paris, but if he is not in Chicago, then he is in Paris. The proposition would not be a true one if Joe could be in both places or in neither place. The same intention is more clearly expressed when father says to little Johnnie, "You can have either ice cream or candy." It should be pointed out that in cases where the disjuncts are actual contradictions, as in "Joe is in Chicago or he isn't in Chicago," though these are exclusive, they result in a contradictory disjunction even when symbolized by a plain wedge, hence the wedge is adequate. The form "P ∨ ∼P" means one and maybe both disjuncts are true but the facts of the case limit the possibility to only one being true.

5. The implicative proposition

An implicative proposition is a proposition in which two sub-propositions are related by a horseshoe ("⊃").

a) THE FORM OF AN IMPLICATIVE PROPOSITION: When any two propositions, P and Q, are related by a horseshoe, the meaning of the compound proposition is that not both can the P be true and the Q be false. Referring back to our symbolization of a contrary disjunctive proposition, we can see that the definition of P ⊃ Q gives the expression the same meaning as ∼(P . ∼Q). Since the latter expression asserts that both disjuncts cannot be true, some further ways of stating the meaning of both expressions would be: either the P is false or the ∼Q is false (∼Q . is false is the same as Q is true); if the P is true, the ∼Q must be false, but if the P is false, the ∼Q is either true or false, i.e., it is undetermined; if the ∼Q is true the P must be false but if the ∼Q is false, the P is un-

determined. Looking at the logical relation of implication between an "A" and an "I" proposition on the square of opposition we find precisely the same relation as that existing between the P and Q when related by the horseshoe. It is
interesting to note, also, that just as the relation between an
"A" and an "I" differed from the other relations on the square
in that it was not symmetrical, so does P ⊃ Q differ from the
other compound propositions forms in that it is not symmetrical. This is indicated by giving distinctive names to the
terms: the first term is called the antecedent and the second
term is called the consequent. In talking about a subcontrary
disjunctive proposition we could say that if either of the disjuncts were false the other would have to be true; we could
just as well say Q ∨ P as P ∨ Q. We are not able to convert an
implicative proposition in the same manner; we must say that
if the antecedent is true, the consequent is true but if the consequent is false the antecedent is false. All of these relations
can be observed on the truth table definition of the horseshoe.

P	Q	P ⊃ Q
T	T	T
F	T	T
T	F	F
F	F	T

b) TRANSLATION OF ORDINARY LANGUAGE: The most common
words in ordinary language that can be translated into the
horseshoe are the words "if" and "implies." Other less frequently used words that can undergo the same translation are
"when," "whenever," and "unless," though the last case requires that the antecedent be denied in order to get a proper
translation. Thus, "unless Joe studies he will fail" means the
same as "if Joe does not study he will fail." It should be remembered, however, that all of these verbal connections usually carry more meaning than what the horseshoe symbolizes.
When we use the words "implies" or "if" in everyday speech
we usually mean that there is a real connection between the
entities referred to by the antecedent and the consequent. Sometimes the real connection is causal as in "if Joe drinks poison
Joe will die"; sometimes these connectives refer to a defini-

tional tie as in "if a thing is rational it is human"; other times logical entailment is meant as when we say "if all men are mortal then some men are mortal."

In all of these cases we feel that if we knew the first proposition were true, we could deduce the second, but we certainly could not deduce "Hitler is dead" from "grass is green" though we can connect the two propositions by a horseshoe. This is possible because the horseshoe only relates truth values; to determine the truth of a horseshoe proposition we need only know the truth of the parts. Despite the fact that the word "if" and others like it carry meanings in ordinary discourse that go beyond the horseshoe, this does not prevent our translating the "if" into the horseshoe since in all of these cases there is one meaning in common—it is impossible for the antecedent to be true and the consequent false. It is only this common meaning that is symbolized by the horseshoe, and it is only this meaning that is important in the evaluation of arguments that contain implicative propositions.

The procedure therefore is to symbolize an "if" proposition as A $\supset$ B and give it the meaning of "P $\supset$ Q." The upshot of this discussion is that though it may seem strange and even paradoxical to say such things as "if grass is green then Hitler is dead," or "P implies Q is true whenever the P is false or the Q is true," these statements are only paradoxical when viewed from a meaning of implication other than that of the horseshoe.

6. The equivalent proposition

Two propositions related by three parallel lines ("$\equiv$") constitute an equivalent proposition.

a) THE FORM OF AN EQUIVALENT PROPOSITION: The meaning of the three parallel lines is that the truth value of the proposition on one side is the same as the truth value of the proposition on the other side. Any two propositions, "P" and "Q" related by a "$\equiv$" are true together and false together. If the P is true, the Q is true, and if the P is false, the Q is false; if the Q is true, the P is true, and if the Q is false, the P is false. From this it can be seen that P $\equiv$ Q has the same meaning as a conjunction of two implicative propositions (P $\supset$ Q) . (Q $\supset$ P). In contrast to the logical equivalence of "all men are mortal" to "no men are immortal," the equivalence of "P" to "Q" cannot be determined by a mere inspection of form, but rather, is discovered by an empirical investigation of the facts. This latter type of equivalence is called "material equivalence."

b) TRANSLATION OF ORDINARY LANGUAGE: The expression in ordinary language, "if and only if," can be translated into the symbol of equivalence. When it is said "if and only if Joe gets a raise will Joe buy a house," the meaning is that if he gets a raise he will buy a house and if he buys a house, then he has received a raise. The expression "P $\equiv$ Q" can be read "P is equivalent to Q," or "if and only if P, then Q." One other ordinary usage should be mentioned: if an implicative proposition happens to be convertible, as is true of a definition, then it can be written "P $\equiv$ Q" rather than as "P $\supset$ Q." An example is "if a thing is a triangle then it is a three-sided plane figure." The situation is analogous to the conversion of an "A" proposition when it is a definition.

7. Summary

The various species of disjunctive propositions as well as the implicative proposition can be summarized by placing them on the same square of opposition used to show the relations among categorical propositions with the same subjects and predicates. This square will then serve as a handy device for remembering the meaning of these compound propositions. Since all of the symbolic logic that we will discuss is simply an extension of these meanings it is vital that they be remembered.

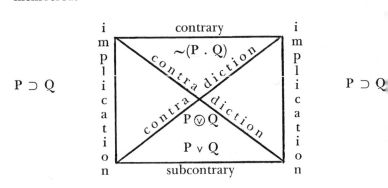

EXERCISE #12: COMPOUND PROPOSITIONS

Assuming the ordinary truth value for the sub-propositions in the following exercise, proceed according to these steps: 1) symbolize the propositions (use A, B, C, etc.); 2) state whether each compound proposition is true or false.

1. Adams is a famous American name and Ralph Jones discovered America.

2. Not both did Columbus discover America and Washington become the first president of the United States.

3. Either Washington was the first president of the United States or Columbus discovered America.

4. Either the first letter of this sentence is typed or it is written in longhand.

5. If Columbus discovered America then New York is not a large city.

6. If and only if Jones discovered America is New York a large city.

7. If Columbus did not discover America then New York is not a large city.

8. Unless Columbus discovered America then Washington was the first president of the United States.

9. Columbus discovered America but New York is not a large city.

10. Either Jones discovered America or New York is a small city.

11. If the person who painted *The Last Supper* was a man then he may have been a father.

12. If the person who painted *The Last Supper* was a woman then she may have been a father.

13. Either the person who painted *The Last Supper* was not a man or Florence is in Italy.

14. If the author of *War and Peace* was a man then he may have become a mother.

15. If the author of *War and Peace* was a woman then she may have been a mother.

16. Jones discovered America and New York is not a small city, or *The Last Supper* was painted by a man.

17. If either Jones discovered America or Columbus discovered America, then New York is a small city.

18. If Jones' discovering of America implies New York is a small city, then *War and Peace* was written by a woman.

19. Either Columbus discovered America and New York is not a small city, or Jones discovered America and New York is not a large city.

20. If Columbus discovered America, then either New York is a large city and *War and Peace* was written by a woman, or Hitler was a Greek.

Chapter VI

THE COMPOUND SYLLOGISM

Though there are many kinds of deductive arguments involving compound propositions, the compound syllogism, a syllogism in which one or more of the propositions are compound, is one of the fundamental types of elementary arguments using compound propositions. In contrast to the procedure followed in handling the categorical syllogism where rules of validity were used, in the case of the compound syllogism validity will be assessed by means of valid forms. These valid forms can be stated verbally as rules of inference, but it is far easier to work with them as forms when evaluating irregular arguments. The notion of form for the compound syllogism will be explained first and then a list of some valid forms will be presented and justified.

1. The meaning of form in the compound syllogism

For the compound syllogism as for the categorical syllogism, an argument is valid because of its form alone. By form, in the case of the compound syllogism, is meant the relation that exists between the truth values of the propositions in the argument. If the meanings of the various compound propositions are kept clearly in mind, the problem of validity becomes extremely simple. Consider, for example, the following argument: "if Joe drinks poison, then Joe will die soon. Joe is drinking poison, hence Joe will die soon."

As we discovered in the last chapter, the first premise is asserting that the antecedent cannot be true and the consequent false; since the second premise asserts that the antecedent is true, we know that the truth of the consequent necessarily follows as a conclusion. Any argument that has this form, .e., in which the second premise affirms the antecedent will necessarily imply that the consequent can be inferred as a conclusion; any argument with this form will be valid regardless of the particular content of the argument. We can symbolize this form as "P ⊃ Q, P therefore Q" and say that any argument that is a substitution instance of this form, *i.e.*, that can be substituted for this form, is a valid argument. Though the argument "~A ⊃ B, ~A therefore B" happens to have a negative content for the antecedent of its first premise, it still is considered a substitution instance for our valid form since the relation between the first and second premise is the same as in the valid form—the second premise is affirming the antecedent of the first premise. It would be redundant to list as further valid forms: "~P ⊃ Q, ~P therefore Q"; "~P ⊃ ~Q, ~P therefore ~Q"; "P ⊃ ~Q, P therefore ~Q" since all of these have the same form as our original valid form. Following from this discussion, of the six arguments below, the three on the left are valid and the three on the right are invalid. *A straight line is used to separate premises from the conclusion.*

A ⊃ B	A ⊃ ~B	~A ⊃ ~B	A ⊃ B	A ⊃ B	~A ⊃ ~B
A	A	~A	~A	~A	A
B	~B	~B	~B	B	B

2. Valid forms of the implicative syllogism

The implicative syllogism, a syllogism in which the first premise is an implicative proposition and the second premise and conclusion are categorical propositions, has two valid forms, the first of which we have already used to illustrate the notion of form.

$$P \supset Q \qquad P \supset Q$$
$$P \qquad\qquad \sim Q$$
$$Q \qquad\qquad \sim P$$

a) VERBAL EXPLANATION OF THE VALID FORMS: The valid forms of the implicative syllogism can be determined by a careful examination of the meaning of an implicative proposition. If what we mean by an implicative proposition is that the ante cedent cannot be true and the consequent false, and if a second premise asserts that the antecedent is true, then clearly the consequent must be affirmed in the conclusion. Also, if the second premise asserts that the consequent is false, then the antecedent cannot be true, *i.e.*, it must be false. The two valid forms can be formulated as a verbal rule that also yields a helpful memory aid: "an implicative syllogism is valid only when the second premise affirms the antecedent (AA) or contradicts the consequent (CC)." It is also the case that the consequent must be affirmed in the conclusion of the first valid form and the antecedent contradicted in the conclusion of the second valid form but it is rather unnecessary to have to say this; the important part of any compound syllogism is the relation of the second premise to the first premise. It would indeed be unusual to find an argument like the following, though it is, of course, invalid: "if Joe drinks poison then he will die soon; Joe is drinking poison, hence he will not die soon."

In contrast to the two valid forms, if the second premise asserts that the antecedent is false no necessary conclusion follows since the consequent could be either affirmed or contradicted in a conclusion; if the consequent is affirmed in the second premise, again no necessary conclusion follows because the antecedent could be true or false under this condition. It is only when an "if" is stated as "if and only if," or when the "if" introduces a definition that it can be written as "$P \equiv Q$" and a syllogism constructed that would be valid in all four forms. An intuitive examination of a set of clear examples may illuminate this discussion. For the following possible combinations of premises, only the *first* and *fourth* will produce a necessary conclusion, hence they are the only ones that will yield valid arguments:

1. If Rex is a horse then he is an animal.
   Rex is a horse.
2. If Rex is a horse then he is an animal.
   Rex is not a horse.
3. If Rex is a horse then he is an animal.
   Rex is an animal.
4. If Rex is a horse then he is an animal.
   Rex is not an animal.

b) TRUTH TABLE EXPLANATION OF THE VALID FORMS: Although it is possible to use truth tables to check the validity of any compound argument, the method becomes far too cumbersome to use when dealing with extended arguments (see the truth table for the dilemma at the end of this chapter). Our concern here is to use truth tables to vindicate the basic valid forms that we are going to use to evaluate arguments. The procedure is similar to the use of analogies as a method of proof but is much simpler because of the use of abstract forms. The key notion behind both analogies and the truth table is that if an argument can be made to have true premises and a false conclusion it is invalid; if not, it is valid.

1. SHORT TRUTH TABLE METHOD: This short method provides a clear, simple method for testing an implicative syllogism. The method is to fill in a false value for the conclusion and then try to fill in true values for the premises; if this can be done, the argument has an invalid form. The assignment of truth values must be consistent, i.e., if the conclusion is a "Q" and it is made false, then a "Q" in the premise must be false and a "∼Q" must be true. Using this procedure on the following four possible implicative syllogisms reveals that numbers one and four are valid while numbers two and three are invalid. It is possible, of course, to make the first premise of numbers one and four true, but if this is done we will be forced to make the second premises false. We cannot get both premises true together and have the conclusion false; hence these are valid arguments.

1)	T	F		2)	F	T
	P ⊃ Q	F			P ⊃ Q	T
	P	T			∼P	T
	Q	F			∼Q	F
3)	F	T		4)	T	F
	P ⊃ Q	T			P ⊃ Q	F
	Q	T			∼Q	T
	P	F			∼P	F

2. THE TRUTH TABLE INSPECTION METHOD: The procedure here is to make a reference column of all possible combinations of truth values of P and Q, string the argument across the top of the truth table, and then fill in the truth values of the argument according to the reference column. When this is done, a simple inspection will show whether there is any instance of the premises being true and the conclusion false. If there is such an instance, then the argument is invalid; if there is not, then the argument is valid. The first argument form below turns out to be an invalid form because the second line has true premises and a false conclusion; the second argument form is valid because the only place where the premises are true is in the first line, and here the conclusion is also true:

P	Q	P ⊃ Q	Q	P
T	T	T	T	T
F	T	T	T	F
T	F	F	F	T
F	F	T	F	F

P	Q	P ⊃ Q	P	Q
T	T	T	T	T
F	T	T	F	T
T	F	F	T	F
F	F	T	F	F

3. THE COMPLETE TRUTH TABLE METHOD: To use this method a new idea must be introduced. Any deductive argument can always be phrased as an implicative proposition in which the antecedent is the premise or premises and the consequent is the conclusion. To say "P, therefore Q" is to say "if P then Q." This has been implicit in our analysis even in talking about the categorical syllogism; we might have phrased a categorical syllogism as an implicative proposition by saying "if all men are mortal and Socrates is a man, then Socrates is mortal." This is possible because both an implicative proposition and a deductive argument are making the same truth claim, namely, that it is not the case that the first part (premises or antecedent) is true and the second part (conclusion or consequent) is false.

If we were to take a truth table of an implicative argument in which there is no instance of the premises being true and the conclusion false, and then add a column that states the premises and conclusion as an implicative proposition, obviously there would only be truth symbols for the implicative proposition. We can say therefore that any argument that when stated as an implicative proposition has only truth symbols is a valid argument. The following is an example of the procedure we have been describing:

P	Q	P⊃Q	P	Q	[(P⊃Q) . P]⊃Q
T	T	T	T	T	T
F	T	T	F	T	T
T	F	F	T	F	T
F	F	T	F	F	T

3. Valid forms of the subcontrary disjunctive syllogism

The subcontrary disjunctive syllogism is a deductive argument in which the first premise is a subcontrary disjunctive proposition and the second premise and conclusion are categorical propositions. The two valid forms of this type of argument are:

$$\begin{array}{cc} \text{P v Q} & \text{P v Q} \\ \underline{\sim\text{P}} & \underline{\sim\text{Q}} \\ \text{Q} & \text{P} \end{array}$$

a) VERBAL EXPLANATION OF THE VALID FORMS: Again an examination of the meaning of a subcontrary disjunctive proposition will point out why only the above two forms are valid. If what is meant by such a proposition is that at least one of the disjuncts is true, then if a second premise asserts that one of the disjuncts is not true, we know the other disjunct must be asserted to be true. If the second premise were to affirm one of the disjuncts, then, since "at least one" leaves open the possibility of both being true, we cannot know whether the other disjunct is true or false, *i.e.*, no necessary conclusion follows. The valid forms can be stated as a verbal rule: "a subcontrary disjunctive syllogism is valid only when the second premise contradicts one of the disjuncts." Of course, the other disjunct must be affirmed in the conclusion but this follows rather mechanically since a person would hardly argue that "Joe is either brave or foolhardy and since he is not brave, he must not be foolhardy." There will be no special consideration given to a contradictory disjunctive syllogism but it might be pointed out that if the word "or" is used in an exclusive sense and is translated into the circle-wedge, then an argument would be valid in all four forms; it would then be possible to affirm one of the disjuncts in a second premise and deny the other disjunct in the conclusion. Looking at the four possible combinations of premises we can see that when the word "or" is used in the inclusive sense it will produce a necessary conclusion only in the second and fourth examples:

1. Either Joe is very smart or he studied hard.
   Joe is very smart.

2. Either Joe is very smart or he studied hard.
   Joe is not very smart.

3. Either Joe is very smart or he studied hard.
   Joe studied hard.

4. Either Joe is very smart or he studied hard.
   Joe did not study hard.

b) TRUTH TABLE EXPLANATION OF THE VALID FORMS: We do not intend to go through the three types of truth tables for each of the four possible forms of the subcontrary disjunctive syllogism, but instead we will use the complete truth table for one of the valid forms and for one of the invalid forms as an illustration of the method. The first form below is a valid one and the second is invalid:

P	Q	P v Q	~P	Q	[(P v Q) . ~P] ⊃ Q
T	T	T	F	T	T
F	T	T	T	T	T
T	F	T	F	F	T
F	F	F	T	F	T

P	Q	P ∨ Q	P	∼Q	[(P ∨ Q) . P] ⊃ ∼Q
T	T	T	T	F	F
F	T	T	F	F	T
T	F	T	T	T	T
F	F	F	F	T	T

4. Valid forms of the contrary disjunctive syllogism

A contrary disjunctive syllogism has as its first premise a contrary disjunctive proposition and its second premise and conclusion are categorical propositions. There are two valid forms of this kind of argument:

$$\sim(P \cdot Q) \qquad \sim(P \cdot Q)$$
$$\underline{P} \qquad\qquad\quad \underline{Q}$$
$$\sim Q \qquad\qquad\quad \sim P$$

a) VERBAL EXPLANATION OF THE VALID FORMS: The meaning of a contrary disjunctive proposition is that the two disjuncts are not both true. This being the case, if we know, through a second premise, that one of them is true, the other must be false. On the other hand, if the second premise asserts that one of the disjuncts if false, then since "not both true" leaves open the possibility that both are false, we cannot know whether the other disjunct is true or false, *i.e.*, no necessary conclusion follows. The valid forms may be stated verbally as "a contrary disjunctive syllogism is valid only if the second premise affirms one of the disjuncts." Again it must be said that though the conclusion must "follow through" this is relatively unimportant; no sane person would argue that "Joe can't both play all night and get good grades and since Joe plays all night, he must get good grades." Using a clear verbal example, it is obvious that of the four possible combinations of premises, only the first and third would produce a necessary conclusion:

1. Not both can Joe play all night and get good grades. Joe plays all night.
2. Not both can Joe play all night and get good grades. Joe does not play all night.
3. Not both can Joe play all night and get good grades. Joe gets good grades.

4. Not both can Joe play all night and get good grades.
   Joe does not get good grades.

b) TRUTH TABLE EXPLANATION OF THE VALID FORMS: Using the complete truth table form for one of the valid forms and one of the invalid forms, we find the first of the following forms is valid and the second is invalid:

P	Q	~(P . Q)	Q	~P	[~(P . Q) .	Q] ⊃	~P
T	T	F	T	F			T
F	T	T	T	T			T
T	F	T	F	F			T
F	F	T	F	T			T

P	Q	~(P . Q)	~Q	P	[~(P . Q) . ~Q] ⊃		P
T	T	F	F	T			T
F	T	T	F	F			T
T	F	T	T	T			T
F	F	T	T	F			F

5. The dilemma

The dilemma is one of the most frequently used forms of syllogistic deductive argument, particularly in debate situations, hence it should be listed among our valid forms. A United States Senator, a few years ago, used the following dilemma in attacking one of his colleagues: "if the Senator believes it when he says the state department is full of communists, then he is mentally incompetent, and if he does not believe it when he says it, then he is morally vicious. Either he believes it when he says it or he doesn't; hence, either he is mentally incompetent or he is morally vicious." The form of the dilemma is that the first premise is a conjunction of two implicative propositions, the second premise is a subcontrary disjunction of either the two antecedents of the first premise or of the contradiction of the consequents (the example above does the former), and the conclusion is a subcontrary disjunction of the consequents or of the contradiction of the antecedents as the case may be.

If the two disjuncts of the conclusion are the same proposition, as in the fourth example below, then it can be written as a categorical proposition. The validity of the dilemma can be seen when it is recognized as a combination, in a sense, of two valid implicative syllogisms; when a second premise says that at least one of the antecedents is true, it must follow that at least one of the consequents is true. If the second premise were to affirm the consequents or deny the antecedents in a subcontrary disjunctive, no necessary conclusion would follow.

Because of its simplicity, the form of the dilemma, as for most of the basic argument forms, is usually maintained; hence the practical mode of criticism is to attack the truth of the premises. For the dilemma, this means escaping through the horns by asserting that there are other alternatives than those stated in the second premise, or an escape can sometimes be made by taking the dilemma by the horns and denying that one or both of the implicative propositions in the first premise are true. A few of the varieties of the dilemma form are given below and an inspection type truth table presented for the first dilemma listed:

1. $(P \supset Q) . (R \supset S)$
   $\underline{P \lor R}$
   $Q \lor S$

2. $(P \supset Q) . (R \supset S)$
   $\underline{\sim Q \lor \sim S}$
   $\sim P \lor \sim R$

3. $(P \supset Q) . (\sim P \supset R)$
   $\underline{P \lor \sim P}$
   $Q \lor R$

4. $(P \supset Q) . (R \supset Q)$
   $\underline{P \lor R}$
   Q

P	Q	R	S	$P \supset Q$	$R \supset S$	$(P \supset Q) . (R \supset S)$	$P \lor R$	$Q \lor S$
T	T	T	T	T	T	T	T	T
F	T	T	T	T	T	T	T	T
T	F	T	T	F	T	F	T	T
F	F	T	T	T	T	T	T	T
T	T	F	T	T	T	T	T	T
F	T	F	T	T	T	T	F	T
T	F	F	T	F	T	F	T	T
F	F	F	T	T	T	T	F	T
T	T	T	F	T	F	F	T	T
F	T	T	F	T	F	F	T	T
T	F	T	F	F	F	F	T	F
F	F	T	F	T	F	F	T	F
T	T	F	F	T	T	T	T	T
F	T	F	F	T	T	T	F	T
T	F	F	F	F	T	F	T	F
F	F	F	F	T	T	T	F	F

EXERCISE #13: COMPOUND SYLLOGISMS

ymbolize the following arguments (use A, B, C, etc.). If the
rgument is valid, write the form that validates it; if invalid,
rove the invalidity by the short truth table method:

1. If war is declared then the enemy country will be invaded.
   War is not declared. Therefore, the enemy country will
   not be invaded.

2. Either he is indifferent or he is forgetful. He is not forgetful, therefore he must be indifferent.

3. Not both can the United States fight a war and lose no
   lives. The United States is fighting a war. Therefore, the
   United States is losing lives.

4. If this number is divisible by two then it is even. This
   number is not divisible by two, therefore it is not even.

5. Either he will study or he will go to the movies. He went
   to the movies. Therefore, he did not study.

6. The president has fulfilled his election promises and since
   it was known that if he fulfilled them he would be re-
   elected, it follows that he will be re-elected.

7. Either Zeke is a dog or he is a cat. He is a dog, hence
   he is not a cat.

8. If Ruth is either ill or tired, then she will stay home. Ruth
   is either ill or tired, hence she will stay home.

9. Unless this number is divisible by an even number it is not
   even. Since this number is divisible by an even number
   it is even.

0. The rumor is that coach Pigskin is out of a job. This piece
   of gossip is based on the fact that the school had a losing
   football record and it is well known that Pigskin had to
   win or he was through.

1. When fraternities become more fraternal, race prejudice
   will decline on college campuses. Since race prejudice is
   declining on college campuses, it follows that fraternities
   are becoming more fraternal.

2. It seems to be impossible for John to devote his life to
   helping backward people and at the same time to making
   a fortune. Since John made a million dollars, it must be
   that he has not devoted his life to helping backward people.

13. It looks as though the foreign automobile manufacturer are better engineers or the American manufacturers ar not concerned with putting out a well-designed, economica car. Since the American auto makers are not concerne with these ends, it must be that the foreign manufacturer are not better engineers.

14. Not both can we keep a dog and not have fleas. We hav fleas so we must be keeping a dog.

15. If Dick studies correctly, he will not fail and he will no get a low grade. Dick studies correctly, so he will not fai and he will not get a low grade.

16. If a woman is good-looking, higher education is super fluous and if she is not, it is inadequate. But either woman is good-looking or she is not. Therefore eithe higher education for women is superfluous or it is inade quate.

17. If you say what is just you will be hated, and if you sa what is unjust you will be hated. But either you say wha is just or you say what is unjust. Therefore you will b hated.

18. If a woman is good-looking, higher education will increas her charm and if she is not, it will give her an attraction c its own. But she must be either good-looking or not. Ther fore higher education will either increase her charm c give her an attraction of its own.

19. If it is true then his friend didn't lie and if it is true the his girl didn't lie. However, either his friend or his gi lied, therefore it isn't true.

20. If Sena then dorut, and if mala then calas. Either doru or calas, hence either Sena or mala.

Chapter VII

IRREGULAR COMPOUND ARGUMENTS

It is now time to return to the argument that generated Part II on symbolic logic: "Joe was not invited or else he was detained. If he were detained, he would call the hostess. Ruth says he was invited, hence he will call the hostess." This argument is called irregular in the sense that it does not pretend to be an instance of any of the syllogistic forms so far discussed nor of any of the elementary argument forms to be discussed, and this being the case, such an argument cannot be evaluated by simply matching it against a valid form. The argument can be handled by a truth table but the process would be at least as long as the one used to illustrate the dilemma and hence not very practical.

Our alternative plan will be to reduce such an argument to a series of elementary arguments from which the conclusion will follow if the argument is valid. In order to do this with mechanical ease, a few more elementary valid forms of argument as well as some logical equivalences must be introduced. After these two tasks have been accomplished, a systematic procedure for evaluating irregular arguments will be presented.

1. Some further elementary valid forms

The four additional valid forms to be explained are introduced because of their usefulness in manipulating symbols for mechanically evaluating irregular arguments. They are all simple enough to need no lengthy defense, hence only a short verbal explanation will be given with a truth table proof for the two most complicated of the forms.

a) <u>CONJUNCTION</u>: The form of a conjunctive argument is 'P,Q therefore P.Q." The comma is an ordinary English punctuation symbol used to indicate that the P and the Q symbolize two separate propositions; if each is true when separated, then a conjunction of the two will be true. By the use of this form it will now be possible to take any two propositions and join them together as a conjunction. This might be very useful as in the following argument, for example: "(A . B) ⊃ C, A, B, hence C." By joining the A and the B of the second and third premises to form a conjunction we would have "(A . B) ⊃ C, (A . B), hence C." This we can see is an instance of an implicative syllogism.

b) SIMPLIFICATION: Since a conjunction asserts that both conjuncts are true, if the conjunction is true, then one of the conjuncts is true. If the proposition "grass is green and snow is white" is true, then the proposition "grass is green" is true. There are two forms of this argument: "P . Q therefore P" and alternatively, "P . Q therefore Q." It would be necessary, in order to evaluate the following argument, that the second premise be simplified to an "A": "A ⊃ B, A . D hence B."

c) ADDITION: The argument form called "addition" allows us to add any proposition to a given true proposition by the use of the wedge and get a true proposition as a result. The form of this argument is: "P therefore P v Q." This looks somewhat strange at first glance, but certainly if we know that "P" is true we can assert that at least one disjunct in the expression "P v Q" is true. If the proposition "Columbus discovered America" is true, then the proposition "Columbus discovered America or Lassie is a Martian spy" is a true proposition. This argument form would be needed to evaluate the following argument: "(A ⊃ B) . (C ⊃ D), A, hence B v D." Knowing that we can add a "C" to the "A" of the second premise by the use of the wedge will allow us to see the argument as a dilemma. A complete truth table proof of this form follows:

P	Q	P	P v Q	P ⊃ (P v Q)
T	T	T	T	T
F	T	F	T	T
T	F	T	T	T
F	F	F	F	T

d) THE PURE IMPLICATIVE SYLLOGISM: This type of implica-
e syllogism is called "pure" because it is constructed out of
ree implicative propositions. It has the form "P⊃Q, Q⊃R,
erefore P⊃R." It has a sort of chain effect that would be
ustrated by saying "if Rex is a collie, then Rex is a dog; if
ex is a dog, then Rex is an animal; hence, if Rex is a collie,
en Rex is an animal." The validity of this form is shown
the following truth table:

P Q R	P⊃Q	Q⊃R	P⊃R	[(P⊃Q).(Q⊃R)]⊃(P⊃R)
T T T	T	T	T	T
F T T	T	T	T	T
T F T	F	T	T	T
F F T	T	T	T	T
T T F	T	F	F	T
F T F	T	F	T	T
T F F	F	T	F	T
F F F	T	T	T	T

2. Logical equivalences

In addition to our list of valid forms, it is convenient to
ve a number of logical equivalences for help in the evalua-
n of irregular arguments. To see that the argument form
⊃ Q , ~Q ∨ R, therefore P ⊃ R" is a form of the pure impli-
tive syllogism it is necessary to know that "~Q ∨ R" is
gically equivalent to "Q ⊃ R." Two propositions are equiv-
nt when they have the same truth value and they are log-
lly equivalent when the equivalence can be determined by a
ere inspection of the meanings of the propositions. For ex-
ple, "P ≡ Q" is true only in the selected cases when the
and the Q actually have the same truth values as determined
some empirical investigation, but "P ≡ ~(~P)" is always
ue—the very meaning of the propositions indicates that they
st have the same truth values.

A distinction is customarily made between these two kinds
equivalences by calling the first type "material equivalences"
d the second type "logical equivalences" or "tautologies."
ough these logical equivalences are similar to the valid
ms in their dependence upon the meanings assigned to the

various compound propositions, there is an important di
ference which should be understood. A valid form only go
one way—if we have P . Q we can infer P, but if we have P
cannot infer P . Q. In the case of equivalences the inferen
goes two ways—if we have P we can infer $\sim(\sim P)$ and if we ha
$\sim(\sim P)$ we can infer P. The various equivalences will
given a verbal explanation and illustration and then the mo
difficult ones will receive a truth table proof.

a) EQUIVALENCES BETWEEN DIFFERENT PROPOSITIONAL FORM
Though these equivalences have already been implicit in o
definitions of the various compound propositions, they w
now be stated explicitly.

1. $(P \supset Q) \equiv \sim(P . \sim Q)$. There should be no problem he
since when the implicative proposition was defined it w
defined as "not both can the P be true and the Q be false" a
this is exactly what is asserted by $\sim(P . \sim Q)$. In each case, if t
P is true, the Q must be true, and if the Q is false, then the
must be false. A verbal example is "if Joe drinks poison th
he will die" is equivalent to "not both can Joe drink pois
and not die." Coining a translation rule would result in sa
ing "an implicative proposition is equivalent to a contra
disjunctive proposition when the consequent is denied in t
disjunction."

2. $(P \supset Q) \equiv (\sim P \lor Q)$. One way of seeing the equivalen
is through recognizing that in each case, if the P were tru
the Q would be true, and if the Q were false, the P wou
be false. The implicative proposition is saying that not bo
can the P be true and the Q be false, which is another w
of saying that either the P is false or the Q is true and this
what the disjunctive proposition is asserting. An ordina
English example of the equivalence would be changing "if yo
try then you can do the exercise" to "you are not trying or yo
could do the exercise." A translation rule can be formulat
for this equivalence by saying "an implicative proposition
equivalent to a subcontrary disjunctive proposition when t
antecedent is denied in the disjunction."

3. $\sim(P . Q) \equiv (\sim P \lor \sim Q)$. If a contrary disjunctive asse
that not both disjuncts are true, another way of saying this
to state that either the one disjunct is false or the other

false. For each proposition, if the P is true, the Q is false and
if the Q is true, then the P is false. Using a loose verbal example for the sake of clarity, the equivalence might be stated
as "pay attention or leave the room" is the same as "you can't
dawdle and stay in the room." (Not both can you not pay attention and not leave the room.) A rule of equivalence between the two forms would be "a contrary disjunctive and a
subcontrary disjunctive are equivalent when the subproposi-
tions in one are denied in the other."

4. **Summary:** An inspection type truth table can summarize
the equivalence between the three types of compound propositions by showing that all three are true together and false
together, *i.e.,* they have the same truth values:

P	Q	$P \supset Q$	$\sim P \vee Q$	$\sim(P . \sim Q)$
T	T	T	T	T
F	T	T	T	T
T	F	F	F	F
F	F	T	T	T

b) EQUIVALENCES BETWEEN PROPOSITIONAL FORMS OF THE SAME
TYPE: As well as having equivalences among the different types
of compound propositions, there are equivalences between two
propositions of the same type; thus, there are conditions under
which, for example, an implicative proposition is equivalent to
another implicative proposition.

1. $(P . Q) \equiv (Q . P)$. Each proposition has the same sub-
propositions and each is asserting that both sub-propositions
are true, so clearly the two are equivalent in meaning. A rule
can be phrased saying that a conjunction is equivalent to a
conjunction when they have the same conjuncts and they are
converted. A truth table would be identical for each proposition. Since the two conjunctions are equivalent, it follows that
the contradictions of each one would be equivalent in meaning, *i.e.,* two contrary disjunctions with the same sub-propositions will be equivalent when the sub-propositions are converted; thus, $\sim(P . Q) \equiv \sim(Q . P)$. It should be mentioned
that the ordinary language sentence "Mary took poison and
Mary died," uses the word "and" to express a causal con-

nection and this proposition cannot be symbolized by the dot and cannot be converted.

2. $(P \lor Q) \equiv (Q \lor P)$. In similar vein, each proposition has the same sub-propositions and is making the same assertion so each has the same meaning. To say "either Joe studies or Joe is brilliant" is the same as saying "either Joe is brilliant or Joe studies." Two subcontrary disjunctions with the same sub-propositions are equivalent when the sub-propositions are converted.

3. $(P \supset Q) \equiv (\sim Q \supset \sim P)$. In contrast to the above two equivalences, this equivalence not only converts the sub-propositions but also contradicts each one. The process is the same as the one called "contraposition" when dealing with categorical propositions. The meaning of an implicative proposition, that not both can the P be true and the Q be false, asserts that if the P is true the Q must be true, and if the Q is false the P must be false; but it does not say that if the Q is true the P must be true. From the proposition "if Mac is a dog then Mac is an animal" we can infer the proposition that "if Mac is not an animal then Mac is not a dog," but we cannot make a simple conversion and infer that "if Mac is an animal then Mac is a dog." The situation is the same as that found in handling a categorical "A" proposition; we can get a contrapositive but we cannot convert an "A" proposition. A truth table with the various possibilities shows why the contrapositive is equivalent whereas the simple converse is not equivalent:

P Q	P⊃Q	Q⊃P	~Q⊃~P	(P⊃Q) ≡ (~Q⊃~P)	(P⊃Q) ≡ (Q
T T	T	T	T	T	T
F T	T	F	T	T	F
T F	F	T	F	T	F
F F	T	T	T	T	T

c) EQUIVALENCES BASED ON CONTRADICTING A CONTRADICTION: The following equivalences are all based upon the notion that if two propositions are related as contradictories, it is possible to make them equivalent by contradicting either one of the propositions.

1. $P \equiv \sim(\sim P)$. The contradiction of P is $\sim P$. Obviously we

could make them equivalent by placing a "$\sim$" before the P. What is not so obvious, but yet is clear enough, is that they can be made equivalent by placing a "$\sim$" before the $\sim$P. The idea seems to be the ordinary commonplace that two negatives make a positive. To say a book is "not not red" is to say "it is red."

2. $\sim(P \supset Q) \equiv (P \cdot \sim Q)$. Since an implicative proposition asserts that the P cannot be true and the Q false, the contradiction of the implication would assert that the P is true and the Q is false; the only place on a truth table of an implicative proposition where it is false is where the P is true and the Q is false. To take a verbal example, a person who says "if you jump you will fall" will be contradicted by your jumping and not falling. Looking carefully at equivalence "a1" above, we can see that it is achieved by taking the contradictories "P $\supset$ Q" and "P $\cdot \sim$Q" and contradicting the latter proposition. What we are now doing is taking the same contradictories and contradicting the former proposition. Not only can we verbally contradict "P implies Q" by saying "P and not Q," but we can do it by saying "it is not the case that P implies Q," or "P implies Q is not true." The latter two versions would be ways of reading the expression "$\sim(P \supset Q)$." A truth table proof of the equivalence follows:

P	Q	P $\supset$ Q	$\sim$(P $\supset$ Q)	P $\cdot \sim$Q	$\sim$(P $\supset$ Q) $\equiv$ (P $\cdot \sim$Q)
T	T	T	F	F	T
F	T	T	F	F	T
T	F	F	T	T	T
F	F	T	F	F	T

3. $\sim(P \vee Q) \equiv (\sim P \cdot \sim Q)$. The reasoning behind this equivalence is the same as for the one above. The contradiction of "P $\vee$ Q" is "$\sim$P $\cdot \sim$Q," hence an equivalence can be formed by contradicting the latter expression as was done, though with different content, in "a3," or by contradicting the former expression as we are now doing. Verbally, we might say that the proposition "it is not true that Joe is either bright or lucky" means the same as the proposition "Joe is not bright and Joe is not lucky." Another version of the same proposition

would be "Joe is neither bright nor lucky." The equivalence can be shown on a truth table as follows:

P	Q	P ∨ Q	~(P ∨ Q)	~P . ~Q	~(P ∨ Q) ≡ (~P . ~Q)
T	T	T	F	F	T
F	T	T	F	F	T
T	F	T	F	F	T
F	F	F	T	T	T

3. Procedures for evaluating irregular arguments

By an irregular argument is meant a compound argument that does not claim to be an instance of any argument form on our list of valid forms. Since an irregular argument does not claim to conform to our list, it cannot be matched against the list and simply labeled valid or invalid. What must be done here is similar to what was done for a sorites; propositions that are implicit must be made explicit and used to form a series of elementary valid arguments and equivalences from the last of which the final conclusion follows. To do this is to present a formal proof that the argument is valid. If this cannot be done, then an attempt can be made by means of a shortened truth table to prove the argument is invalid.

Both of these methods are needed since each method is only effective for one of the jobs. The fact that a person is not able to prove an argument valid by means of the valid forms does not prove that the argument is invalid—it may only indicate a lack of skill in constructing the proof; an inability to make the premises true and the conclusion false by the truth table method does not prove the argument is valid—again it may only indicate a lack of skill in using the method. However, if an argument is proved valid by the valid forms then it is valid, and if an argument is proved invalid by the truth table method then it is invalid. After discussing each of these techniques, there will be some final remarks on the handling of arguments with inconsistent premises.

a) PROCEDURE FOR PROVING VALIDITY: The example we will use is the one already mentioned twice: "Joe was not invited or else he was detained. If he were detained he would call the hostess. Ruth says he was invited, hence he will call the

hostess." In attempting to prove the validity of such an argument it is well to adopt and regularly use an orderly method
of procedure. One method of proceeding involves the following steps:

1. Symbolize the argument, number each premise, and place
the conclusion to the right of the last premise and separated
from the premise by a diagonal Line:

1. ~ A ∨ B
2. B ⊃ C
3. A / C

2. Construct an argument by using one or more of the
premises and drawing a conclusion according to any of the
valid forms or equivalences on our list. The conclusion should
be stated first and numbered to follow the last premise of the
original argument. After the conclusion, there should be a
listing of the numbers of the premises used in constructing the
argument. The premises are to be followed by a semicolon
and then a statement of the valid form or equivalence that
justifies the argument. The result might look like this:
4. B 1,3; P ∨ Q, ~P/Q. An alternative deduction might have
been: 4. A ⊃ B 1; (P ⊃ Q) ≡ (~P ∨ Q). There is no mechanical
method for determining what deduction to make; the aim is to
produce a conclusion that will be useful in proving the final
conclusion of the argument and the only aids are a firm grasp
of the valid forms and equivalences, practice, and in the case
of the more difficult arguments, some native ingenuity. Sometimes it is helpful to figure out the propositions from which
the final conclusion can be deduced and then see if these
premises can be deduced from the original premises. Thus,
one might see that "C" could be deduced from "B⊃C, B"
and that since we have the "B⊃C," if we could only get the
"B" we could get the final conclusion of "C." It is usually
good practice to begin the deductions by using a categorical
proposition if there is one among the premises.

3. Construct another argument using any of the original
premises as well as any proposition that has been proved. If
this argument has as its conclusion the conclusion of the
original argument, then the argument has been proved valid,

i.e., you have deduced the conclusion from the original premises plus two valid forms or equivalences; if you cannot construct such an argument keep trying until you can or until it is clear that this cannot be done. Basically the process of proof is akin to the process of solving puzzles—there may be much trial and error until skill is attained through practice. The final appearance of our proof might be the following:

$$1. \sim A \lor B$$
$$2. \quad B \supset C$$
$$3. \quad A \;/\; C$$
$$4. \quad B \;\; 1,3; \; P \lor Q, \; \sim P \;/\; Q$$
$$5. \quad C \;\; 2,4; \; P \supset Q, \; \; P \;/\; Q$$

An alternative proof that is just as good though less elegant because of more steps would be:

$$1. \sim A \lor B$$
$$2. \quad B \supset C$$
$$3. \quad A \;/\; C$$
$$4. \quad A \supset B \;\; 1; \; (P \supset Q) \equiv (\sim P \lor Q)$$
$$5. \quad A \supset C \;\; 4,2; \; P \supset Q, \; Q \supset R \;/\; P \supset R$$
$$6. \quad C \;\; 5,3; \; P \supset Q, \; P \;/\; Q$$

b) <u>PROCEDURE FOR PROVING INVALIDITY</u>: The argument we will use is: "if Joe is stupid and lazy then he is not college material. If Joe is not college material he is not officer material. Joe is officer material, therefore he is not lazy." Symbolized, the argument would look like the following:

$$1. \quad (A \cdot B) \supset \sim C$$
$$2. \sim C \supset \sim D$$
$$3. \quad D \;/\; \sim B$$

If an attempt were made to prove this argument valid it would end in failure; we could prove "$\sim(A \cdot B)$" and this should tell us that unless we have an "A" we cannot prove the "$\sim B$," and we do not have an "A" nor can we get one. In this situation, the short truth table method should be attempted since if we can make the premises true and the conclusion false, this would prove the argument is invalid. One way of doing this would be:

$$
\begin{array}{ll}
 & \text{F T}\qquad\ \ \text{F} \\
\text{T } 1. & (A . B) \supset \sim C \\[4pt]
 & \text{F}\qquad\ \text{F} \\
\text{T } 2. & \sim C \supset \sim D \\[4pt]
 & \ \ \text{T}\quad\ \text{F} \\
 & 3. \quad D / \sim B
\end{array}
$$

c) <u>PROCEDURE FOR PROVING INCONSISTENCY</u>: Taking a very simple argument for purposes of illustration, let us see what could be done with the following: "A . ∼A / B." At first glance it looks ridiculous, yet we will find that it is impossible to assign truth values to prove it invalid. Obviously, if we make "A" true, then "∼A" will be false and if we make "∼A" true, the "A" will be false. On the other hand, if we try to prove the argument valid we find it can be done in the following steps:

$$
\begin{array}{ll}
1. & A . \sim A / B \\
2. & A \quad 1; P . Q / P \\
3. & A \vee B \ 2; P / P \vee Q \\
4. & \sim A \ 1; P . Q / Q \\
5. & B \ 3,4; P \vee Q, \sim P / Q
\end{array}
$$

At this point we might have observed that the contradiction of the conclusion could be proved by going through the same steps, but adding a "∼B" instead of the "B" in step three. Any time contradictions show up in a proof this is an indication that the argument is valid but that at least one of the premises is false. The notion behind all of this is similar to what we found in defining an implicative proposition—from a false proposition anything follows. Given "A . ∼A" one can validly prove the moon is made of green cheese. Whenever an argument "smells self-contradictory," the contradiction of the conclusion should be proved as well as the conclusion.

4. Summary

For the sake of convenience of reference, there follows a complete list of the valid forms and logical equivalences we are using:

Valid Forms

1. P ⊃ Q, P / Q
2. P ⊃ Q, ~Q / ~P
3. P ∨ Q, ~P / Q
4. P ∨ Q, ~Q / P
5. ~(P . Q), P / ~Q
6. ~(P . Q), Q / ~P
7. (P ⊃ Q) . (R ⊃ S), P ∨ R / Q ∨ S (plus varieties)
8. P , Q / P . Q
9. P . Q / P
10. P . Q / Q
11. P / P ∨ Q
12. P ⊃ Q, Q ⊃ R / P ⊃ R

Logical Equivalences

13. (P ⊃ Q) ≡ ~(P . ~Q)
14. (P ⊃ Q) ≡ (~P ∨ Q)
15. ~(P . Q) ≡ (~P ∨ ~Q)
16. (P . Q) ≡ (Q . P)
17. (P ∨ Q) ≡ (Q ∨ P)
18. (P ⊃ Q) ≡ (~Q ⊃ ~P)
19. P ≡ ~(~P)
20. ~(P ⊃ Q) ≡ (P . ~Q)
21. ~(P ∨ Q) ≡ (~P . ~Q)

EXERCISE #14: LOGICAL EQUIVALENCES
(For Chapter Seven, section II)

a) For the following pairs of propositions: 1) symbolize (A, B, C); 2) state whether they are equivalent:

1. If it rains I will stay home.

   Either it does not rain or I will stay home.

2. If we practice we will win the game.

   If we do not practice we will not win the game.

3. Not both can a person be a teacher and make a million dollars.
   Either a person is not a teacher or he makes a million dollars.

4. Either he is a genius or he is simply crazy.
   If he is not crazy then he is a genius.

5. If war is declared, then most of the youth will have to serve.
   Not both can war be declared and most of the youth not serve.

6. If we don't go we will not see the parade.
   Either we don't see the parade or we go.

7. If he does not play this Saturday he will quit the team.
   Either he plays this Saturday or he will quit the team.

8. A fellow can't both be impolite to the girls and expect them to want his company.
   Either a fellow is polite to the girls or he can't expect them to want his company.

9. If the White Sox win the pennant, then the World Series will be played in Chicago.
   If the World Series is played in Chicago, then the White Sox won the pennant.

10. Cleveland won the American League Championship and the Giants won the world series.
    The Giants won the world series and Cleveland won the American League Championship.

11. The Russians must either want peace or they are deceiving people.
    The Russians are either deceiving people or they want peace.

12. Either he isn't well or he isn't trying hard.
    If he is well, then he isn't trying hard.

13. The psychologist can't both say all reasoning is rationalization and then use reason to show that the statement is true.
    If the psychologist says all reasoning is rationalization, then the psychologist cannot use reason to show that such a statement is true.

14. If you touch a frog you will get warts.

   If you don't touch a frog you won't get warts.

15. Chicago is in the United States and London is in England.

   If Chicago is in the United States, then London is in England.

b) If the proposition "A ∨ B" is true, what can be inferred about the truth or falsity of the following propositions?

   1. A ⊃ B
   2. ~A ⊃ B
   3. B ∨ A
   4. ~B ⊃ A
   5. ~(A . B)
   6. A . B
   7. ~(~A . B)
   8. B ⊃ A
   9. ~(~A . ~B)
   10. ~A . ~B

EXERCISE #15
IRREGULAR COMPOUND ARGUMENTS
(For Chapter Seven, section III)

Symbolize the following arguments (use A, B, C etc.) and give a formal proof of validity or a short truth table proof of invalidity as the case may be:

1. If wealth were increasing, then there would be more great fortunes. If there were more great fortunes, there would be great incentive to work hard. It seems to be the case that there can't both be great incentive to work hard and a high income tax. Since there is a high income tax, it follows that wealth is not increasing.

2. Fredonia is either a democracy or it is run by a few men in power. Since Fredonia can't both be a democracy and have great inequalities of wealth, and the latter situation is true of Fredonia, it must be true that Fredonia is run by a few men in power.

3. If pleasure is the goal of life, then our great religious

leaders were either very ignorant or were liars. If either of these alternatives were true, then all of our knowledge about their characters would be false, but the latter is not the case. Hence, pleasure is not the goal of life.

4. If the Bears won today's game and the Rams lost their game, the Bears would win the championship. Since the Bears did not win the championship I guess the Bears must have lost their game.

5. If it were cold outside, the man who is walking down the street would be wearing his earmuffs. If it were slippery, the man across the street would have sanded his walk. If the man walking down the street were wearing his earmuffs, or if the man across the street had sanded his walk, I could observe it from here. But I can't observe it from here. Therefore, it is neither cold nor slippery.

6. If the Dodgers are to win the pennant, then either the other teams will have to fold up or the Dodgers will have to continue playing winning ball. It isn't likely that the other teams will fold up; therefore, it isn't likely that the Dodgers will win the pennant.

7. If there is an obstruction on the line or the block signal is red, the train will stop before it reaches the bridge. The train does not stop before it reaches the bridge. Therefore, there is no obstruction on the line.

8. If the U.N. tried to win the Korean war quickly, it would be over in a week. We couldn't both end the war in a week and stay out of a war with China. Since we are keeping out of a war with China, it follows that we are not trying to win the Korean war quickly.

9. If Joe is brilliant or studies hard, he will make good grades. Joe didn't make good grades, so the statement that he is brilliant or studies hard can't be true.

10. If you do God's will, you will work hard and if you work hard, you will have a lot of money. If you have a lot of money, you will live the life of luxury. Therefore, if you live in luxury, you are doing God's will.

11. Zeno argued: In order to move, a body must either move in the place where it is or it must move in a place where it is not. But a body cannot move in the place where it is,

and it is obviously impossible for a body to move in a place where it is not. Therefore, it is impossible for a body to move at all.

12. Had either the president or the secretary of defense been notified, a statement would have been issued and a special cabinet meeting called. Had a statement been issued, there would have been a special newscast. There was, however, no special newscast. So the president could not have been notified.

13. The doctor gives large sums to charity, or his reputation is overrated. It is not the case that he receives a small salary and at the same time gives large sums to charity. Therefore, if the doctor's reputation is not overrated, then he does not receive a small salary.

14. If it rains or no one cares to come, then the sale is a failure. The sale is not a failure. Therefore, it is not the case that no one cares to come.

15. An argument heard shortly after the war, went as follows: Great Britain cannot be sincere in proclaiming that she is struggling for the preservation of democracy in the world while she at the same time is morally justified in denying the democratic processes to India. It can readily be seen that Great Britain is sincere in proclaiming that she is struggling for the preservation of the democracies in the world. Thus, she is not morally justified in denying the democratic processes to India.

16. If I am going to get a good grade, I must study hard and if I am going to be on the team I must practice long hours. If I practice long hours and study hard, I will get sick. Since I can't afford to get sick, I must either not get good grades or not be on the team.

17. If John attends class and studies, he will pass his course. Either John fails or he graduates. If John graduates, then he will get an interesting job and make a good living. John did not get an interesting job. Therefore, he did not attend class and he did not study.

18. If the theory of evolution is true, there will be fossils of extinct forms. If the account of creation in Genesis is true, there will not be fossils of extinct forms. Thus, if the

account of Genesis is true, the theory of evolution is false.

19. The president stated that Smith should be removed from office because of his conviction for income tax evasion. The law states that officers should be ousted upon conviction of an infamous crime. The president pointed out that income tax evasion has been declared a felony and the law holds that all felonies are infamous crimes.

20. If Bobby is a girl, Bobby could be a mother. If Bobby is not a girl, Bobby could be a father. Bobby could neither be a mother nor a father. Therefore, Bobby is a syllogism.

EXERCISE #16: REVIEW OF SYMBOLIC LOGIC
(For Chapters Five, Six and Seven)

Symbolize the following arguments (use A, B, C, etc.) and give either a formal proof of validity or a short truth table proof of invalidity as the case may be:

1. Not both can Mary take clear notes and not understand the subject. Since Mary did not take clear notes, she must not understand the subject.

2. If that is a mail train, then it isn't an express. It isn't the mail train, therefore it is an express.

3. Either I'm sleepy or I didn't study enough. I know I have studied enough so I must be sleepy.

4. If Joe studies he will get a good mark. Joe studies, hence he will get a good mark.

5. If the price of food increases, the poor will starve; and if the price of fuel increases, the poor will freeze. But either the price of food will increase or the price of fuel will increase. Therefore, either the poor will starve or the poor will freeze.

6. If Joe is drafted, he will have to live away from home. Joe can't both live away from home and eat well. Therefore, either Joe is not eating well or he isn't drafted.

7. If it had been a burglar last night, then something would have been taken. It was either a burglar or some kid playing a prank. Since nothing was taken, it must have been a kid playing a prank.

8. If he had either studied or had some talent, then he would have been a success in his recital. He wasn't a success in his recital so he didn't have talent but he did study.

9. If either Ty Cobb or Ted Williams are great ball players, then Roy Smalley is not. If there is a single standard for great ball players, then Babe Ruth and Bob Feller can't both be great. But if Roy Smalley is not, then Ruth and Feller are great. Also, it is true that Ted Williams is great. Therefore, there is no single standard for great ball players.

10. If all of the nations of the world get under a common government, then there will be no war. If there is not war, then there will be no need for bomb shelters. But either bombs will have to be eliminated or there will be a need for bomb shelters. Therefore, we can't both have a common government for all the nations in the world and not have bombs eliminated.

PART III

INDUCTION

In the discussion up to this point, we have been concerned with deduction and the problem of validity. Deduction will tell us the consequences of our beliefs and will help inject consistency into our beliefs but this method will not necessarily result in truth unless we start with true premises. Though we can consider an argument solely from the viewpoint of the correctness of reasoning from the premises to the conclusion, in most practical situations we are also concerned about truth, *i.e.,* with the correspondence of our beliefs to facts. In handling inductive arguments we shall again focus on the problem of reasoning from the premises to the conclusion, but in this case, since the premises are a matter of direct sense experience (though perhaps with complicated apparatus), we will automatically get an assurance of some probability of truth in our conclusion if our observations are accurate and our reasoning correct. Inferences from sense experience can take any one of three directions, each of which results in one type of inductive argument. From an experience of sheets that are well-laundered, we can: 1) generalize that all sheets done by this laundry will be done well; 2) reason by analogy that the laundry would do towels well; 3) reason to a hypothesis that will explain the experience, namely, the laundry uses a certain kind of soap. An analysis of these three types of inductive argument is the chief task of the following two chapters.

Chapter VIII

INDUCTION: SIMPLE FORMS

By an inductive argument is meant an argument in which the premise or premises are derived from some direct sense experience and on the basis of this it is claimed that the conclusion is probably true. This chapter will deal with the simpler forms of induction, namely generalization and analogy, that expand our experience of a set of similar facts to a fact not yet experienced. Thus, after perceiving that a laundry has frequently done a good job on our sheets, we might generalize that probably all sheets done by the laundry will be nicely laundered, or we might reason by analogy that newly laundered towels will probably be done well. Though our main concern is with induction, a preliminary section will consider induction along with some alternative accounts of ways of attaining truth.

1. Ways of knowing

The problem of getting propositions that are true resolves itself into four major answers, each of which has had and still has its defenders.

a) DEDUCTION: Though a deductive proof always operates by assuming the premises are true, an attempt might be made to prove that the premises of a particular argument are true by deducing them from another set of premises. It is clear that this procedure only gives rise to the same problem for the new deductive argument. In the argument "all rabbits are cowards and all cowards are despised, therefore all rabbits are despised," are the premises true? We might try to prove the first premise by arguing that "all creatures that run from men are cowards and all rabbits are creatures that run from men, therefore all rabbits are cowards." How do we know these premises are true? In the face of this situation, the deductionists or rationalists, have gone on to say that if a total set of deductive arguments about the world are mutually consistent, this indicates that they are yielding truth. Two difficulties with this coherence view of truth are that when two or more coherent schemes are presented there seems to be no way of choosing between them, and further, the theory does not agree with the facts concerning how we do actually know such propositions as "grass is green" or "many crows are black"—to wit, by observation.

b) INTUITION: According to the intuitionist view, the mind is capable of apprehending truth immediately and without the need of proof. This theory is frequently joined with a rationalist view and then results in the notion that the premises are intuited as true and then, through reason, we deduce further truths. The propositions that are intuited are regarded as self-evident, *i.e.,* they are supposed to carry their evidence with them and need no support beyond the intuition that discerns their truth. The difficulty with this position is again that when intuitions conflict there is no way of settling the issue. As a result, most moderns refuse the term "self-evidence" to propositions like "reality is material" and limit its use to tautologies such as "all quadrupeds are four-footed." Though the latter proposition is true, propositions of this sort will not solve our problem since they mainly tell us about the meanings of words and do not furnish new factual truth about the world. Also, even the extreme intuitionist would not claim that he knows most crows are black by intuition.

c) AUTHORITY: Another possible way of getting true propositions is through the testimony of some person or persons. The form of an argument from authority is "Joe says 'X' is true, therefore 'X' is true." This kind of argument probably furnishes most of the factual truth we possess, yet, because it must rest on some other method by which the authority gets his information, it is no real solution to our problem. We might accept the proposition "the human infant has gill slits" because biologists testify to it, but we only do this because we realize that some biologists have made direct observations.

However, because of the practical importance of arguments from authority and because such arguments can be better or worse, it is well to examine the criteria used in their evaluation. The criteria are similar to those we will find used to evaluate inductive arguments, but in the case of authority they are applied to a person rather than to empirical data. Again, like inductive arguments the conclusion of an argument from authority must always be qualified by the word "probable." When the premise of an argument is the authority of some individual or individuals, the problem of correctness becomes a problem of evaluating the authority. If the testimony comes from a person who 1) is competent in that field; 2) has access to facts; 3) is unbiased; and 4) if the testimony agrees with other facts and testimony, then the proposition being testified to can be accepted as probably true. The argument above about gill slits would be a case in point.

If an argument from authority is particularly bad in terms of these criteria, then the fallacy of authority is committed. To argue that "Crunchies are probably the most nutritious breakfast food because Home-Run Kelly says this is the case" is to depart from all of the criteria and commit the fallacy. Home-Run Kelly is not an expert on nutrition, he has no access to the facts, he is paid for his testimony, and his testimony conflicts with the claims of other manufacturers of breakfast foods. The best protection against fallacies of this sort is to remember that to speak with authority one must be an authority; this does not necessarily mean having a good body, a pretty face, or a famous name—it means having knowledge about the subject under discussion.

d) INDUCTION: Since none of the positions so far discussed can be justified as primary sources of our knowledge about the world, we are left with the thesis of empiricism, namely, that all knowledge begins with sense experience. The building-blocks of knowledge are the direct reports of a sense experience as in the proposition "this crow is black," and further, the drawing of a conclusion from premises that are direct reports of sense experience, such as in the proposition "all crows are black." In the latter case, there has not been an observation of every crow but some black crows have been observed and from this the conclusion has been drawn that all crows are black. When we argue this way we are using an inductive argument.

1) THE NOTION OF PROBABILITY: As noted in the first chapter of the text, all inductive arguments should have their conclusions qualified by the word "probable." Since the conclusion of an inductive argument is based on the experiences formulated in the premises, and since experience is never "all in," the conclusion can never be known with certainty. By the word "probable" we are indicating that the truth of the conclusion is never beyond question; though we may feel practically certain that "all men are mortal," this statement does not have the certainty that accompanies the conclusion of a valid deductive argument in which the premises are true. Of course, its certainty is only hypothetical since the premises may not be true. However, if all men are mortal and Socrates is a man, it cannot be the case that Socrates is not mortal. It can be the case, though it is extremely unlikely, that there is a man who is not mortal. In all inductive arguments, the truth of the premises renders the conclusion only probable, and as the evidence stated in the premises accumulates or declines, the probability of the conclusion being true increases or diminishes as the case may be. The probability of an inductive conclusion is always relative to the evidence. It should also be observed that though the conclusion of an inductive argument can never be proved true, the conclusion can be proved false by a single piece of evidence; it would take only one non-black crow to disprove the proposition that all crows are black.

2) RELATION OF INDUCTION TO DEDUCTION: Induction represents a fundamental mode of knowing and arguing just as does deduction. Neither method is to be thought of as superior or inferior—they are simply two different methods, each with its own particular use. If we were concerned with seeing the implication of our beliefs about human equality and in the humanity of the Negro, we would use deduction and draw the conclusion that the Negro should be treated as an equal. If we want to find out if a box of strawberries is good, we would look at samples from the box and then make an inductive generalization. In the total enterprise of human knowledge, deduction and induction work together—we want to both get the facts and see what the facts imply. If we are to have sound deductive arguments we must start with premises that ultimately have been justified by the method of induction. If

we are to see the implications of the conclusions of our inductive arguments, we must construct valid deductive arguments. In the method of science we have a model for the coöperation of deduction and induction—the scientist investigates, generalizes, and formulates hypotheses, but just as fundamental are his mathematical deductions of the consequences of his hypotheses, observations, and generalizations.

2. Generalization

The basic type of simple inductive argument is one in which the conclusion is a generalization. What is essentially involved in this kind of argument is that on the basis of some cases known through experience, an inference is made to a proposition that refers to the whole collection of cases. We observe the connection of the property "black" to *some* crows, and then reason to the conclusion that probably *all* crows are black. The facts are evidence for the conclusion because they are instances of the generalization. Underlying this inductive leap from cases that we have examined to cases that we have not examined is the assumption that the examined cases are representative of the whole class of cases.

a) SINGLE INSTANCE GENERALIZATIONS: In some cases where there is a great deal of information indicating that the class of objects is homogeneous, one or a few examined cases will allow us to generalize about the whole class of objects. For example, since water is known to be homogeneous, one taste of a glass of water will tell us about the taste of the rest of the glass of water. Likewise, when a generalization fits into a well-established network of generalizations, only one case may be needed to establish the new generalization. On the basis of well-established generalizations about the human body and the nature of iodine, one case would be sufficient to establish that iodine is a poison.

b) CRITERIA FOR EVALUATING ISOLATED GENERALIZATIONS: When a generalization is neither based on a known homogeneous class nor is it part of an established set of generalizations, then it is necessary to observe certain rules to maximize the chance that the cases examined are representative, *i.e.,* that they are a fair sample of the total class of cases. Since crows are not homogeneous nor is there any reason why they should be black, a case in point would be "all crows are black." The following rules are the criteria that determine whether such an isolated generalization is justified or not:

1. *The sample should be large.* Obviously, the more cases examined, other things being equal, the better is the chance that the cases examined are representative of the entire class of cases. To justify the conclusion that all of the peaches in the crate are firm would entail feeling and looking at many of the peaches since we know that peaches are not a homogeneous class of objects, and we do not know of any established generalizations that link peaches with firmness.

2. *The sample should be random.* This test is immediately indicated when we consider that we would not be satisfied if the grocer picked out a great number of peaches and let us examine them. We don't want a "stacked deck." By this we mean that each peach should have as good a chance as any other peach to be included in the sample. A particularly flagrant evasion of this rule is observed in advertisements that say "99% of the doctors endorse our product." By neglecting the factor of randomness, it is possible to get a 100% endorsement for any product.

3. *The sample should include all sub-classes.* When a class of objects has rather clearly defined sub-classes or strata, there should be a numerous and random sampling of each sub-class. We know that there is a tendency to put the worst fruit at the bottom and also the bottom tends to get squashed. To make a just estimate of the quality of the whole crate it would be necessary to look at all parts of the crate.

c) LIMITED GENERALIZATIONS: Not all generalizations are universal in character. In ordinary life and in the social sciences, many of our generalizations state that "most A is B" or have a statistical formulation such as "50% of A is B." Neither of these types of generalizations involves any new principles, though statistical generalizations are usually based on a rather mathematically complicated description of the sample.

d) FALLACY OF HASTY GENERALIZATION: The fact that many generalizations of daily life are limited suggests that universal generalizations are difficult to justify in this area. The fallacy of hasty generalization results from generalizing far too broadly on the basis of the evidence given, and universal generalizations are particularly prone to commit this fallacy. Familiar examples are "all red-heads have bad tempers," "all women are fickle," "all men are brutes," "all Spaniards are passionate," "all Englishmen are without a sense of humor," etc. The fallacy can also be committed with a "most" statement such as "most beautiful girls are dumb." It is this fallacy that lies behind many of our beliefs about national, racial, and religious groups and engenders many of our conflicts—we know a few obnoxious Slobovians and generalize about many, most, or all Slobovians.

3. Analogy

A second simple form of inductive argument, argument by analogy, starts from a generalization about certain objects or events and then on the basis of known resemblances between these objects or events and other objects or events, extends the generalization to include the new cases. On the basis of our experience of having sheets well-laundered, we make an implicit generalization that most or all sheets are well-laundered, and then on the basis of resemblances between sheets and towels, it is reasoned that towels will be well-laundered. Since an argument by analogy is dependent upon a supporting generalization, this type of argument is frequently regarded as a species of generalization, rather than as a basic type of inductive argument as are generalization and hypothesis. Letting X stand for sheets and Y for towels and with the letters A, B, C, and D representing the characteristics of being cotton, white, flat, and well-laundered, the following diagram indicates the form of an argument by analogy:

X	A	B	C	D
Y	A	B	C	therefore D

a) ILLUSTRATIVE ANALOGIES AND ARGUMENT BY ANALOGY: Before evaluating any argument by analogy, care must be taken to ascertain that it is really an argument and not merely the use of analogy to produce a vivid explanation of some point. We might liken the rules of validity for deductive arguments to machinery that makes shoes: just as putting properly prepared leather into the front end of the machine results in shoes at the other end, so subjecting arguments in standard form to the rules will result in arguments being labeled valid or invalid. Such an analogy may result in clarification but certainly there is no intention of presenting evidence for a conclusion. This use of analogy is assertion and not argument.

b) CRITERIA FOR EVALUATING ARGUMENTS BY ANALOGY: An argument by analogy depends upon three factors: the supporting generalization, points of resemblance, and the lack of serious differences. Each of these factors yields a criterion for evaluating arguments by analogy.

1. *The supporting generalization should be well-justified.* If an argument by analogy moves from one class of events, for example, sheets that are well-laundered, to a new event of the same class, *i.e.,* laundering the next batch of sheets well, the argument will be well-justified if the supporting generalization is well-justified. The proposition "iron rusts" has the same reliability as the proposition "the next piece of iron I see will rust." However, if the argument moves from sheets to towels, in addition to knowing that sheets are well-laundered, the following two criterion must be kept in mind:

2. *There should be many similarities between the objects.* The fact that the sheets and towels are alike in being cotton, white, and flat provides a good basis for arguing that they will be alike in the further characteristic of being well-laundered. If we could add more characteristics that we know they have in common such as size and weight of material, this would add to the worth of the argument. On the other hand, adding a common irrelevant characteristic such as both being bought in Boston would not help the argument at all.

3. *There should be no serious dissimilarity.* If the towels have fancy lacework and the sheets do not, or if the sheets were silk and the towels cotton, then the probability of the argument would decrease. An argument by analogy in which there is a serious dissimilarity is so weak that it is customarily called the fallacy of false analogy. An unfortunate common example would be the following: "I never read the examination papers of my students from the beginning to the end. After all, you don't have to eat a whole egg to tell if it is bad."

c) CRITICAL COMMENTS ON ARGUMENTS BY ANALOGY: Even at best, arguments by analogy are rather weak,—we use the phrase "deceptive analogy"—yet they frequently are the only mode of argument available in the situations of daily life. How, for example, do we pick a restaurant when we are going to dine out? How do we choose books at the library? How do we choose movies to attend? In each case, we have had a good experience in the past and then have reasoned by analogy that the new experience has similarities to the past and hence will also be a good experience. The chief value of argument by analogy is that it can point out possibilities which can then be treated as hypotheses and further investigated. Ben Franklin noted a number of resemblances between electrical sparks and lightning and was led to wonder if lightning could possibly be a form of electricity. He did not rest in this argument by analogy but regarded it as a hypothesis to be tested. He conducted a test with his kite-and key-experiment and found that lightning was electrical.

EXERCISE #17: AUTHORITY
(For Chapter Eight, section I)

For the following arguments from authority, underline or write out the conclusions and then criticize the arguments in terms of the criteria mentioned in the text:

1. The Flash car is the best car because their salesman says it is the best car.

2. Cigarettes do not cause cancer. We have the authority of the private research staff of the cigarette companies for this statement.

3. It is likely that God exists, since every theologian believes that God exists.

4. Public health insurance would be bad for the political and economic well-being of our country. Almost all of the doctors hold to this view.

5. The mean distance from the earth to the sun is about 93 million miles. We can accept this statement because the astronomers agree that it is probably true.

6. Almost all of the economists agree that tariffs protect in-efficiency. Therefore, it is probably true that tariffs have this effect.

7. The great majority of political scientists say that the short ballot would improve our political processes. Therefore, this is probably the case.

8. Attendance at Church or Sunday School is a valuable factor in the training of youth, for it is recommended strongly by all our leading industrialists and business men.

9. The Truman administration's policies were all wrong, for they have been condemned by General MacArthur, one of the greatest military geniuses of all time.

10. It is wrong for America to belong to the United Nations Organization, for Washington, the Father of Our Country, specifically warned us against entangling alliances.

EXERCISE #18: GENERALIZATION
(For Chapter Eight, section II)

For the following arguments to a generalization, underline or write out the conclusions and then criticize the arguments in terms of the criteria mentioned in the text:

1. Three times during the past month I have read about paroled convicts who committed new crimes. This proves that "once a criminal, always a criminal."

2. A popularity contest is being conducted at a school with an expected vote of 500 students. A sample is taken by asking the students in the library on a Friday evening whom they favor and 15 out of the 25 people in the library say they will vote for candidate "A." You conclude that "A" will win.

3. A person makes a bowl of popcorn, notices the big fluffy kernels on the top and wonders if the whole bowl consists of such nice popcorn. He decides to get a sampling by shaking the bowl and finds he always gets nice corn at the top. He concludes that all of the corn in the bowl is big and fluffy.

4. There is probably great public support for increasing the

tax levy for the schools because every member of the P.T.A. favors such a proposal.

5. To predict the next election when a vote of about 60,000,000 is expected, a sample is taken. Phone calls are made at random to 3,000,000 people and it is found that candidate "A" is favored by 2,000,000 and candidate "B" is favored by 1,000,000 people. The conclusion is drawn that candidate "A" will win.

6. We have observed thousands of crows and every one has been black. This proves that all crows are black.

7. No major league baseball player has hit more than 61 home runs in one season. Therefore, it is likely that no player ever will hit more than 61 home runs in one season.

8. I have three sisters with red hair and each one has a hot temper. I guess all red-heads have hot tempers.

9. There is a jar of black and white beans. After a thorough mixing, a handful of beans is taken out and it is found that there are 23 black beans and 25 white beans in the sample. It is concluded that probably half of the beans in the jar are black.

10. My girl has started to go out with other boys. All girls are fickle.

EXERCISE #19: ANALOGY
(For Chapter Eight, section III)

For all arguments by analogy, underline or write out the conclusions and then criticize the arguments in terms of the criteria mentioned in the text:

1. Since children must be cared for by their parents, it follows that backward nations should be cared for by the more advanced nations.

2. The chicken we ate last week was cooked in wine and tasted delicious. The same should be true if we cook our chops in wine tonight.

3. There are great similarities between the earth and the other planets. For example, they all revolve around the sun, receive their light from the sun, and are subject to gravitation. From these similarities we conclude that the

other planets, like the earth, are inhabited by living creatures.

4. Mr. Adam has a new Flash V-8 and gets excellent mileage from it. Miss Eve just bought the same model car, so she probably will get good mileage.

5. The popular belief that mental processes cause bodily changes is a myth. They have no more influence upon the body to which they belong than the smoke from a locomotive has upon the movement of the train.

6. "Like as the waves make towards the pebbled shore, so do our minutes hasten to their end."

7. "Look at the color of my fingers after smoking cigarettes. Can you imagine what my lungs must be like?"

8. "True, Governor Salmon appointed some men to office who have betrayed their trust. Some 1,960 years ago a man appointed 12 men to be his disciples, and one betrayed him. But do we as Christians say that Christ failed his duty?"

9. "The biggest and best companies in the world seek out the men best equipped for their top jobs," said the athletic director of Podunk University. "So why shouldn't the universities go after the best athletic talent?"

10. Mrs. Smith, a second grade teacher in Chicago, added that "knowledge implanted in seemingly barren ground may take longer to sprout, but it always grows hardier when it does."

Chapter IX

INDUCTION: COMPLEX FORMS

Instead of starting, as did generalization and analogy, with a set of similar facts, an argument to a hypothesis begins with a set of *dis*similar facts and then attempts to explain them by stating their cause. An example would be: "The door is locked, the shades are drawn, nobody answers the bell; therefore, the people are probably not at home." In this argument, each fact formulated in the premises is different from every other fact and together they pose a problem. The conclusion is a hypothesis that explains the facts by stating their cause. The discussion in this chapter will begin with an analysis of the structure of an argument to a hypothesis and then present some general criteria for evaluating this kind of argument; after this, there will be an examination of the methods of experimental inquiry that can be used to test hypotheses when it is possible to manipulate and vary the factors involved in an argument.

1. Hypothesis

Though the argument cited above about "the people not being home" may seem reasonable enough for minor everyday decisions, there are occasions, particularly in scientific inquiry, where a more precise estimation of the justification of a hypothesis is demanded. In order to achieve an adequate understanding of the criteria of correctness for an argument to a hypothesis, it will be well to observe a hypothesis functioning as it would in the context of scientific inquiry. The process we call scientific method is based on the use of hypotheses but it also involves the use of deduction, generalization, and analogy as well as specialized and precise tools for observation and measurement.

Crime detection provides a simple illustration of the use of all these aspects of scientific method, and an analysis of a typical case should serve to identify the steps involved in scientific inquiry and also indicate the criteria relevant to the judgment of such an inquiry. The only difference between crime detection and scientific investigation is that the scientist deals with facts that constantly repeat themselves, hence his hypotheses can be generalized and regarded as laws. There is no need to consider this aspect of the problem since it adds nothing to our previous discussion of generalization. Our case is a classic in the field of detective fiction, "The Maltese Falcon" by Dashiell Hammett; the analysis will proceed by moving through the steps of scientific method and then explaining the criteria for evaluating a hypothesis.

a) THE STEPS OF SCIENTIFIC METHOD: The following pattern of steps should not be regarded as a rigid temporal scheme since many times the "later steps" come before the "earlier steps"; however, the pattern serves a useful purpose if it indicates that there are these five distinguishable steps in scientific inquiry. Also, if an argument to a hypothesis is put into this framework it will point out what is to be done when various hypotheses of equal probability are suggested by the original facts. Instead of merely labeling each hypothesis as probable, improbable, etc., we can go through steps 4 and 5, *i.e.*, deduce further facts, and make further tests.

1. *Statement of the problem:* At the beginning of a criminal investigation, as well as of a piece of scientific inquiry, there is a fact or various facts that point to the existence of a problem. Miles Archer, a partner in the detective agency of Spade and Archer, is found shot to death in an alley. This points to a problem which is phrased in the question "Who killed Miles Archer?" The chief concern at this stage of the inquiry is that the problem be clearly stated and that it reflects a genuinely unsettled situation, rather than a state of personal puzzlement. If the problem is correctly stated, *i.e.*, if the right question is asked, then the problem is well on the way to a solution. Many times questions are asked that stop all search for evidence and thus kill the inquiry before it can get started. Examples would be: "Is there an invisible cow in the corner of the room?" "Is my experience of color the same as your experience of color?" There must be some notion of how to answer a question or the question is a foolish one, and,

as is commonly said, "foolish questions get foolish answers."

2. *Collection of facts:* After a problem is recognized, further observations are made and more facts come into view. We are surrounded by a sea of facts that we never notice—it takes a problem or some interest in a situation to notice that there are powder burns around the wound, that the spot where he was killed would be dark even with the moon shining, that there was no evidence of struggle, etc. Some of the facts brought to light would require technical apparatus of the laboratory— path of the bullet, time of death, etc.

3. *Formulation of a hypothesis:* It's because certain facts are puzzling that they set a problem and it's because a hypothesis explains the facts that the puzzlement and the problem are said to disappear. By explaining the facts we mean that the facts could be deduced from a conjunction of the hypothesis and some generalizations. In the light of general knowledge about Miles' liking for the girls, his professional caution about being approached in a dark alley, the cause of powder burns on a wound, the hypothesis is formed that Miles was shot by a girl and specifically, by the girl he was shadowing on a case. The deductive formulation would be "If the girl Miles was shadowing killed him, then in the light of the generalizations stated above, we would expect him to be shot in a dark place and at close range." Since the consequent states the facts and is what can be affirmed, the argument is of course not valid; however, affirming the consequent does lend a certain probability to the antecedent being true. The more facts affirmed in the consequent, the more probable is the antecedent which is the statement of the hypothesis.

4. *Deduction of further facts:* The steps up to this point make an argument to a hypothesis look like any other type of argument in that step #2 states the premise and step #3 states the conclusion. Step #1 is not a part of the argument, but it does serve to emphasize the problematic nature of this type of argument and thus the explanatory relation of the conclusion to the premises. The important point to notice is that most arguments to a hypothesis, and the one at hand is typical, have little justification at step #3. Certainly no judge or jury would give a conviction on such scanty evidence. This is not, however, the end of the story of the justification

of a hypothesis and of scientific inquiry. A hypothesis not only explains the facts that give rise to the problem and other facts that come into view, but a hypothesis implies and thus explains further facts.

So far as the original facts are concerned, there frequently are many hypotheses that seem to explain these facts equally well. It might be that a trusted friend approached Miles in the alley and killed him, or some other girl might have killed him. In such a situation, further facts must be deduced from the hypothesis and particularly facts that would be implied by one hypothesis but not by the others. "If the girl Miles was shadowing killed him, then she would not have a good alibi, she would have a motive, the gun could be traced to her, etc." It is this sort of thing that is referred to when mention is made of the predictive power of a hypothesis. When a scientist predicts an eclipse of the moon, he does it by having a hypothesis about planetary motions and then deducing future positions of the planets from this hypothesis. These can then be checked and the hypothesis verified or disproved.

5. *Verification of the deduced facts:* When observations are made in order to see if the deduced facts really *are* facts, it becomes possible to increase the probability of the hypothesis, decrease it, or even eliminate the hypothesis. If it were discovered that the girl had an iron-clad alibi, she could not have committed the crime. Such a situation would establish a sound deductive argument: "If the girl is guilty then she has no alibi, but she has an alibi; hence she is not guilty." On the other hand, deduced facts that are verified can be added to the facts cited in step #2 and the total set of facts will constitute the premises of the argument. Just as "unobservable facts" could not occur at step #2, so it is useless to deduce consequences from a hypothesis if they cannot be checked by some kind of sense experience. If the girl is guilty, we might have deduced that her conscience would bother her, but there does not seem to be any ready way of observing this phenomenon even if it did occur.

b) CRITERIA FOR EVALUATING AN ARGUMENT TO A HYPOTHESIS: Predicted facts may have a greater psychological impact and persuasiveness than the facts that gave rise to a hypothesis, but logically they are all on the same level, hence the facts in step #2 and in step #5 can be lumped together for the purpose of evaluation of an argument. Further, it should be understood that an argument to a hypothesis is never a simple matter of evaluating just the argument presented—it is always a matter of considering the probability of one hypothesis as against other alternative explanations of the problem. Though an argument can be criticized because the problem is not a real one or because the observations are not accurate, the important criteria that bear directly on the reasoning involved are the following three:

1. One hypothesis is more probable than other hypotheses if it explains more facts than the others do. If hypothesis "A" explains facts "1—2—3—4", hypothesis "B" explains facts "1—2—3", hypothesis "C" explains facts "2—3—4", then hypothesis "A" is the most probable of the three.

2. One hypothesis is more probable than other hypotheses if it has less diverging facts. Some diverging facts such as a lack of fingerprints on the gun, or a failure to trace the gun to the girl, would weaken the hypothesis of the girl's guilt, but a diverging fact such as an "iron-clad" alibi would ruin the hypothesis.

3. One hypothesis is more probable than other hypotheses if it is simpler than the others. If Miles' death were to be explained by the hypothesis that a strange woman killed him and then manufactured the evidence that pointed to the girl he was shadowing, this would be possible but too complicated to be very probable; in effect, this explanation is using two hypotheses. By "simple" is not meant "easy to understand," but rather that there are fewer variables. Einstein's scientific hypothesis explaining the movement of objects may be difficult to comprehend, but it is simple in the sense that it operates with a single space-time continuum rather than with an independent space and an independent time as did Newton's hypothesis. The notion behind this criterion resembles the old saying "don't send two boys to do the work of one."

c) SOURCE OF HYPOTHESES: Sometimes the five steps of scientific method are spoken of as though they provided a mechanical method for arriving at hypotheses. This is not true; the facts, in themselves, do not point plainly at one hypothesis for all to see. Where a hypothesis comes from is something of a mystery. Mention might be made of intuition, insight, and imagination but one point seems clear—these devices only operate within the framework of a wide background of knowledge. It is this background that contributed the generalizations about Miles' character, etc., that opened the way to the insight that perhaps the client killed Miles. It would seem that a hypothesis is generated by a process of reasoning by analogy from a large background of information. Miles has acted in a certain way towards girls in the past, therefore he probably acted in the same way to this new girl. This analogy hints at the hypothesis that the girl killed him, but only to a person with insight and knowledge.

2. Mill's methods of experimental inquiry

In the case of the murder of Miles Archer, it is not possible to arrange the factors so that the murder would occur many times and the girl be present every time it occurs, nor can we fix things so that when the murder is potential but does not occur, the girl is absent. Since the hypothesis is stating the cause of the murder, and since a cause is a circumstance that is invariably associated with its effect, if the above manipulation could be made it would offer evidence of the girl's guilt.

Sometimes such an experimental environment can be created and when it can the methods of experimental inquiry formulated by John Stuart Mill in the nineteenth century will offer various patterns for manipulating the factors so the evidence will be presented for or against the various hypotheses. Mill's methods thus serve as criteria for evaluating hypotheses. It is perhaps most clear if we regard these methods as deductive patterns for step #4 in the scheme of scientific method; when we cannot deduce new facts from a hypothesis, then we can deduce that the hypothesis will have an invariant connection with the effect it is supposed to explain and perhaps be able to check this deduction. If we got sick after lunching on soup salad, and coffee, we could test each possible cause by deducing that there would be a constant correlation between the cause and the sick people and then testing this deduction.

a) FORMULATION OF MILL'S METHODS: The process of experimental inquiry can be introduced by considering the following situation: a family consisting of father, mother, Bob, Dick, Ruth and Beth are faced with a problem—father, mother, and Dick have broken out with rashes on their faces. What is the cause of the rashes? On the basis of general information about such things, we would not consider as hypotheses the color of their hair, the size shoe worn, etc. but we would consider the food they ate and the things they put on their faces. So far, the analysis is like the analysis of any argument to a hypothesis, but the question now arises—how do we know which hypothesis explains the facts? We know that the fact that a person's fingerprints are on a murder weapon is evidence for the hypothesis that he committed the crime, but is the fact that mother ate berries evidence for the hypothesis that berries caused the rash? If we consider the hypothesis that the girl committed the crime we look for motive, fingerprints, etc.—what do we do if we want to test the hypothesis that berries caused the rash? We will examine three of the five methods of Mill to see how they would answer our question.

1. *The method of agreement:* According to this method, if there is one and only one circumstance common to all instances of a phenomenon, then this circumstance is probably the cause of the phenomenon. We must use the word "probable" because we can never be sure that all circumstances have been considered, and also, our analysis may be too crude and hence lump many factors into one circumstance. Using our example of the family with the rash, the following pattern, with crosses standing for the presence of the different circumstances, would indicate that the soap was probably the cause of the rashes.

phenomena of rash	berries	skin lotion	soap	fruit juice
father	x	x	x	x
mother		x	x	
Dick			x	x

2. *The method of difference:* A statement of this second criterion would be that if there is one and only one circum-

stance present when an instance of the phenomenon occurs
and absent when an instance of the phenomenon does not
occur, this circumstance is probably the cause of the phenomenon. Continuing the same problem, the following pattern
would also point to the soap as probably the cause of the
rashes:

instance of rash	berries	skin lotion	soap	fruit juice
father	x	x	x	x
no instance of rash				
Bob	x	x		x

3. *The joint method of agreement and difference:* This
method has the following statement: if there is one and only
one circumstance common to all instances of a phenomenon
and absent from all instances where the phenomenon does not
occur, then this circumstance is probably the cause of the
phenomenon. It is clear that this method is a combination of
the methods of agreement and difference, and consequently, a
method that gives a considerably higher probability to a conclusion. The following pattern would again point to soap as
probably the cause of the rashes:

instances of rash	berries	skin lotion	soap	fruit juice
father	x	x	x	x
mother		x	x	
Dick			x	x
no instances of rash				
Bob	x	x		x
Ruth	x	x		
Beth		x		x

b) CRITICISM OF MILL'S METHODS: These methods may seem
very stiff but actually they are used easily and frequently,
though perhaps not carefully, in solving many of our everyday problems. When we awaken with a headache it is very
natural to wonder what unique thing we did the night before,

or try to figure out what it is that we do on all of the nights that precede our awakening with a headache. To think this way is to use Mill's methods. Though it has been claimed that these methods are methods of discovery and of proof, it would be more accurate to say that they establish a probability for one hypothesis by eliminating its rivals; the chief value of these methods is to eliminate wrong hypotheses rather than to discover or prove the right hypothesis. The methods are not methods of discovery because the cause must be included in the list of circumstances before it can be "discovered." Neither can the methods prove a hypothesis.

The following criticisms of the argument that "soap caused the rashes because soap is the only circumstance present when the rashes are present and absent when the rashes are absent" bear out this point: 1) The cause may be something not even mentioned, namely, emotional tension. 2) The cause may be a combination of two circumstances, as for example, soap and sensitive skin. 3) The cause may be an ingredient in the soap such as perfume.

c) THE "POST HOC" FALLACY: Though a cause comes before its effect, one thing is not necessarily the cause of another thing because it comes before the other thing. Temporal succession is a necessary element in a causal relation, but it is not a sufficient condition for saying a causal relation exists. In fact, identifying such a situation as a case of causal connection is called the fallacy of *post hoc*. This is an abbreviation of the Latin expression "*post hoc ergo propter hoc*" which means "after this, therefore caused by this." Many of our superstitions about black cats, knocking on wood, breaking mirrors, etc. are examples of this fallacy. We notice a few cases of temporal succession, ignore all other factors, and then say there is a causal connection. If the connection between "black cats" and "bad luck" were justified by Mill's methods, then presumably there would be a causal connection; but even in this case, we would want to find a chain of intermediate events and a theory that would explain the connection. Without such an explanation, both events might be effects of some common cause much as the succession of night and day is the effect of a common cause.

EXERCISE #20: HYPOTHESIS
(For Chapter Nine, section I)

For the following arguments to a hypothesis, put the arguments into the pattern of steps followed by scientific inquiry and criticize the arguments in terms of the criteria mentioned in the text:

1. John and Dorothy were a poor but happily engaged couple. The only occasion for sadness was the fact that John could not afford to give Dorothy an engagement ring. One night as they were sitting in the parlor, John told Dorothy to close her eyes. When she opened them she saw on her finger an engagement ring with a huge diamond. She was troubled but she did not let John know. Later, after John had left for home, she sat and pondered the problem— how could John afford the ring? The thought came—maybe it was a fake diamond. She tried scratching it and looking through it but both tests proved inconclusive. Then she thought about having it evaluated by a jeweler. The next morning she took it to a jeweler and he said it was an excellent diamond. When she got home she found John waiting and her bags packed. He said, "Let's go; we're getting married right away; my aunt died and left me $50,000 dollars." Dorothy sighed with relief for she now knew the answer to her problem.

2. Dr. Breuer's patient was a girl of twenty-one, of a high degree of intelligence. She had developed in the course of her two years' illness a series of physical and mental disturbances which well deserved to be taken seriously. She had a severe paralysis of both right extremities, impairment of vision, nausea when she attempted to drink or eat, the power of speech was diminished, and she suffered from spells of delirium. During these spells, she mumbled words over and over which seemed to indicate that her mind was busy with some kind of associations. The doctor put her under hypnosis and by repeating these words over to her, got her to relate the associations. They all seemed to focus around the situation of a girl at the sick-bed of her father. After relating these fancies, for a few hours she

was restored to a normal life. The conclusion seemed inescapable—the patient suffered from memories.

3. Among the Kuloo Indians there is a legend to the effect that long ago white men visited their shores. The white men came in long boats driven by sails and many oars. The men wore metal helmets with curved horns on the sides. Professor Smith explains the legend by saying Norsemen visited the Indians in the distant past. Professor Jones objects to this hypothesis on the grounds that there is no material evidence of such a visit. Professor Smith says a tidal wave swept away all of the evidence.

4. Charles Darwin points to the following facts: 1) There are no sharp lines between the species of animals. 2) Upland geese which rarely or never swim have webbed feet. 3) Horses occasionally have stripes on their shoulders. 4) The embryos of mammals, birds, and fish are very much alike. 5) The calf has teeth which never cut through the gums. 6) There are many anatomical similarities between classes of animals—the hand of man, wing of a bat, fin of the porpoise, and the leg of a horse. 7) New varieties of animals have been created by selective breeding. Darwin concludes that species are not immutable but rather, they have evolved from earlier existing species.

5. For days the body had lain in state in the church. Each day thousands of people visited the church to pay their respects to the saintly woman who had dwelled among them for so long. One of these days, with the church filled to overflowing, a strange event occurred—a statue of the Virgin turned forty degrees and faced the coffin. An investigation was made and it turned out that the foundation of the church had shifted and this caused the statue to turn. However, many people believe that God turned the statue.

EXERCISE #21: MILL'S METHODS
(For Chapter Nine, section II)

For the following causal arguments, underline or write out the conclusions and criticize each argument in terms of Mill's methods:

1. How do the ardent feminists explain the fact that Switzerland, the sturdy bastion of peace and freedom in the Western world for 600 years, is the only country remaining in Europe that forbids women to vote in national elections?

2. Dr. Smith in his report mentioned a study of smokers among servicemen in Korea. It was found there was less frostbite among smokers than among nonsmokers.

3. A heartsick mother told of tragedy in her home. She found several paper-back books in her daughter's room. Several days later she surprised her daughter and her school friend having unnatural relations. What caused it? "I sincerely believe," said the mother, "it was only curiosity coming from their leisure reading of this material."

4. Dr. Jones had bad news for women who patronize reducing salons which promise to produce the body beautiful by massage. He told of an experiment he conducted with 60 overweight women, 40 of whom were kept on a low diet, the rest maintaining a normal diet. All were also given vigorous massages on arms and thighs twice a day for ten days. The low dieters lost an average of 23 pounds, Dr. Jones said, the others lost no weight. The massages did not reduce measurements of arms but slightly increased the thigh measurements in both classes.

5. Judge Smith, under questioning by Alderman Jones, cited the case of the one-time boy killer, Howard Long, as an example of a crime caused by comic books. Long, who slew 7-year-old Mary Brown, was an avid reader of comic books, the judge said.

6. Among the 440,000 pupils who received the vaccine only 113 cases of the disease developed, while among the 440,000 pupils who received blank injections, 750 cases of the disease developed. This shows that the vaccine will cause immunity.

7. We had better omit the number "13" in numbering the apartments.

8. After Pasteur had found a vaccine against anthrax, 24 sheep, one goat, and five cattle received the preventive inoculations. An equal number of sheep, goats, and cattle were added to the herd, and all 60 animals were infected

with anthrax microbes. Two days later, all of the unprotected animals were dead or dying, while the vaccinated animals were still in good health.

9. John got intoxicated after drinking whiskey and soda, brandy and soda, rum and soda, and gin and soda. He concluded that he had better stay away from soda.

10. A man took two pieces of ground with similar soil and exposure, put fertilizer on one and no fertilizer on the other. He then planted corn in each piece of ground. Each piece of ground received the same watering and weeding but the ground with the fertilizer produced tall corn and the other ground did not.

EXERCISE #22: REVIEW OF INDUCTION
(For Chapters Eight and Nine)

Identify the type of inductive argument, underline or write out the conclusions, and criticize each argument in terms of its appropriate criteria:

1. We know that vitamin B1 increases the intelligence of rats because of the following experiment: two rats of equal size and weight take the same time to learn a given maze. Rat A and rat B are given the same diet for two weeks, except that rat A is also given small daily amounts of vitamin B1. At the end of two weeks, both rats are taught to run a second maze, and this time rat A learns it in a shorter time than rat B.

2. Communism has taken over American education. Investigators working for the Congressional Committee have brought in tons of evidence. Patriotic college teachers, whose names cannot be revealed, have testified, at great personal risk, that their promotions have been blocked, and their students prejudiced against them, by faculty and administration fellow-travelers who resent their outspoken Americanism. They have even attributed their inability to do research to worry over the leftwing infiltration of their college.

3. I enjoyed the last three books by Snow. The reviews say that his latest book also deals with a significant issue and

shows imagination and feeling so I am sure that I will enjoy it too.

4. Since Marlon Brando's first three movies were excellent, it seems reasonable to think that all of his movies will be excellent.

5. We would hold it a crime if a transatlantic liner were not brought to a stop by a signal of distress from a mere fishing smack. Yet a miner is entombed alive, a painter falls from a scaffold, a brakeman is crushed while coupling cars, a merchant faces financial ruin, and organized society leaves widow and child to bitter want or degradation.

6. I have seen tigers in the zoo, in movies, and in the circus, and all of them have had stripes. Probably all tigers have stripes.

7. The radio announcer ruined Joe Smith's no-hit ball game. How do I know? Well, Joe had a no-hitter going until the ninth inning and then the radio announcer said that Joe had the no-hitter going. As soon as he said this, the man at bat got a hit.

8. A person wondered about the effectiveness of sun tan lotions so he and his friend used different lotions and sat together at the beach for about two hours. His friend got a bad burn but he got a nice tan. He concluded that his lotion was more effective than his friend's lotion.

9. The procedure used in voting for candidates in a nominating convention is quite wrong. Why should the delegates have to stand up and publicly say who they are voting for? If you believe in the secret ballot for regular elections, you should believe in secret voting in a nominating convention.

10. Verdict of the jury: Bruno Hauptmann is guilty of the kidnapping and murder of the Lindbergh baby. The facts are these: 1) The kidnapper's ransom note indicated that the author was a German and Hauptmann was a German. 2) An expert said the notes were in Hauptmann's handwriting. 3) The handwriting on a note left in the nursery after the kidnapping was the same as that on the ransom notes. 4) Hauptmann had $20 of the ransom money in his pocket when arrested and there was $14,600 more con-

cealed in his garage. (Hauptmann said the money was left to him for safe-keeping by a friend named Fisch who since had died.) 5) Though he had only a small amount of money before the kidnapping, after the kidnapping both he and his wife quit their jobs and spent about $35,000 on trips, etc. (the amount of the ransom was $50,000). 6) The man who paid over the ransom money identified Hauptmann as the man to whom he paid the money. 7) The ladder used in the kidnapping was made from lumber from Hauptmann's attic floor and from lumber bought at a company where Hauptmann had worked. Also, Hauptmann was an expert carpenter. 8) The nails used in the ladder had the same small defects as nails found in Hauptmann's house. 9) Paper like that of the ransom notes was found in his home. 10) Ground marks after the kidnapping indicated that the kidnapper might have injured his leg—Hauptmann walked with a cane for a few weeks after the crime. 11) He worked near the Lindbergh home, and an automobile that fit the description of his own car was seen near the Lindbergh home shortly before the kidnapping. 12) He had a criminal record in Germany before coming to the United States. 13) The telephone number and address of the man who was to pay over the ransom money was found written on the back of a closet door in Hauptmann's home. He said he copied it from a newspaper ad., but it never was in a newspaper.

PART IV

SEMANTICS

It is customary to divide logic texts into three sections: deduction, induction, and semantics. In addition, there is usually one chapter dealing with the so-called non-formal fallacies, *i.e.,* fallacies that are not simply the result of breaking the rules of deduction or induction, but rather, are arguments that are so bad that the rules cannot even be applied. Since these non-formal fallacies are basically the result of an inattention to the uses and meanings of language, it seems proper to consider the language problems studied by the semanticists and the topic of non-formal fallacies in a single unified account. The fact that there are two fundamental ways in which language can confuse our thinking leads us to classify non-formal fallacies under two heads: 1) The confusion of the various functions of language leads to a number of specific non-formal fallacies that can be classified under the heading of emotive fallacies. 2) A confusion of meaning in the words and propositions leads to a group of non-formal fallacies called fallacies of ambiguity.

Chapter X

LANGUAGE AND NON-FORMAL FALLACIES

A fallacy is an argument in which an error in reasoning is combined with some degree of persuasiveness. In formal fallacies, such as affirming the consequent in an implicative syllogism, the error lies in the form of the argument and the appeal comes from the close approach to a valid form. Nonformal fallacies ignore the element of a logical relationship between the parts of an argument; they are arguments where the factor of relevance between premise and conclusion is absent. An example would be "Kingstons are America's fastest growing cigarette, therefore they are the best cigarette." When we are given an argument we want the premises to bear on the conclusion, and then our job will be to evaluate the weight of the evidence. In the case of a non-formal fallacy, the premises and the conclusion have nothing to do with each other, hence there is no weight of evidence. This being the case, wherein lies their persuasiveness? Perhaps the best answer is to say that the badness is hidden by the language used; though there is no real relevance of the premises to the conclusion, the language is so misused that it appears as though the relation of relevance does exist. In the example of Kingston cigarettes, the emotional appeal of the language pushes us from premise to conclusion, though there is no logical connection. All of these non-formal fallacies are bad arguments and the only critical effort that is needed is to label them with a name that will indicate the particular kind of irrelevancy that is involved.

1. Functions of language and emotive fallacies

Emotive fallacies are arguments in which the premises are not relevant to the conclusion, yet because the language is used emotively, the arguments seem persuasive.

a) THE FUNCTIONS OF LANGUAGE: Among the semanticists, the people who deal with problems of language, it is customary to speak about language as having three functions. Language can be used *directively,* as in the command "open the window"; *emotively,* as in "my love is like a red, red rose"; *informatively,* as in "all widows are wealthy." Though the purpose of a piece of discourse can frequently be discovered by observing the type of grammatical statement that occurs, this is not always the case. It is not true that all declarative sentences are informative in function, exclamatory sentences emotive, and imperative and interrogative sentences directive. We can use a declarative sentence such as "your party was delightful" and not be intending to give information but merely expressing our feelings. Sometimes we use a declarative sentence not to give information but to direct action, as when a father says to his son "the grass needs cutting." Likewise, the interrogative sentence "how are you?" is not intended to be a directive for a report but, rather, is an expression of friendly feeling. If a parent were to say to a child "stealing is wrong," this might encompass all three functions of language: information is given about the moral quality of stealing, the parent's feeling about stealing is exposed, and there is a directive to the child not to steal. The way to understand the purpose of a piece of discourse is through experience and sensitivity and not through any mechanical procedure.

b) EMOTIVE FALLACIES: Though we need not be so purist as to eliminate all emotionally-tinged words from informative discourse, yet there is a matter of emphasis which indicates that emotive language is most proper in poetry or after hitting one's thumb with a hammer. To ignore this point is to open the door to irrelevancy and one of the various emotive fallacies. The matter or content of the premises is directed at the emotions or prejudices of the audience rather than at their powers of reasoning. *Feeling* pushes the audience along smoothly and easily from the premises to the conclusion even though no logical relation exists. When an argument uses emotionally-tinged words or when the premises consist of popular cliches, then is the time to "stop, look, and listen." The proper response to any of the following fallacies might be—"stop emoting and say something."

1. *Ad Populum:* "John must be guilty of the crime. Look at this bloody knife. Look at this bloody ring. Can you imagine a crime as horrible as this one?" An "ad populum" argument is an appeal to the common emotions of people. In the case cited, the appeal was directed at the emotion of horror by speaking of the bloody nature of the crime, but it might have been aimed at pity by speaking of John's youth and then asking for an acquittal. A familiar device is the placing of John's wife or girl friend on the stand. Not all cases of "ad populum" are put so bluntly but they are all alike in the lack of logical relevance between the evidence and the conclusion, and in the emotional appeal of the premises.

2. *Ad Hominem:* "John must have committed the murder because he is a wastrel who has never worked a day in his life, he beats his wife, and he is always drunk." Since John's character is irrelevant to the issue of whether he committed this particular crime, attacking John's character in the premises is a fallacy and any persuasiveness the argument has is due to its emotional appeal.

3. *Poisoning the Well:* A fallacy similar to the "ad hominem" is committed when reference is made to a person's self-interest being involved in a situation. This would occur if it were argued that "John's statement of his innocence must be false because he would say he was innocent no matter what the situation might be." As we saw in the argument from authority, if a person is biased, *i.e.,* if his self-interest is involved, or if he is untrustworthy, little worth would be given to his testimony; however, this does not mean that his statements must be false—sometimes innocent men truthfully say they are innocent.

4. *Appeal to Force:* "John is guilty of the crime because the mothers of the city say he is and they are all voters in the next judicial election." This, again, is an irrelevancy but the argument might be persuasive in its appeal to the judge's fears about the coming election. Similar arguments offered by pressure groups appear to be persuasive to legislators.

5. *Argument from ignorance:* "John must be guilty since he can't prove his innocence." The argument carries psychological appeal because of the emotional tendency to equate

accusation with guilt unless there is a clear proof of innocence; but of course, guilt must be proved just as much as innocence.

2. Definition and the fallacies of ambiguity

Fallacies of ambiguity are arguments in which the premises are not relevant to the conclusion but, because the meaning of the discourse is not clear, the irrelevancy is not noticed and the argument may appear persuasive. The lack of clarity may be due to faulty grammar or a lack of attention to the meaning of the words used; since grammar is a lengthy subject and is treated extensively throughout the school years, we will devote our attention to the problem of definition which, by custom, has been left in the hands of the logician. Though definition is not a cure-all for the fallacies of ambiguity, knowledge of the principles of definition will bear directly on some of these fallacies and in its emphasis on clarity will have some sharpening effect for all types of ambiguity.

a) DEFINITION: To define a word is to state the meaning of a word. Since words have a double reference in that they refer to things, events, etc. (denotation or extension), and they convey ideas about the things, events, etc. (connotation or intension), "meaning" itself will have at least two meanings. When asked what the word "chair" means we might give examples or point to chairs, or we might say "a piece of furniture used to sit on." In this latter type of definition, the connotative one, the meaning of a word is explained by a phrase that uses a general characteristic (genus—a piece of furniture) and a specific characteristic (differentia—used to sit on). In stating the characteristics, if an attempt is made to conform to ordinary usage, then the resulting definition can be called true or false according to whether it conforms or does not conform to ordinary usage.

However, many times, in the interest of theoretical usefulness, a deliberate departure is made from ordinary usage, and in this case the terms true and false do not apply. This would be the situation for such definitions as "democracy is a way of life," "religion is a matter of ultimate commitment," etc. In either case, the purpose of a connotative definition is to characterize an object so that it can be clearly distinguished from all other objects and thus make for precision in thought.

The customary meaning of "definition" is connotation, and it is for this kind of definition that certain rules have been formulated.

1. *A definition should not be obscure or figurative:* "Heaven is the place where nobody goes" may be interesting, but it does not yield much enlightenment as to the meaning of "heaven." A scientific definition may legitimately be obscure to the layman, but the definition of a word in ordinary use should not be obscure.

2. *A definition should not be circular:* "A celibate is a person in a state of celibacy" is of little help to a person who does not know the meaning of "celibacy." Sometimes this rule is broken by using synonyms such as "coat" and "cloak" or antonyms like "good" and "bad."

3. *A definition should state important characteristics associated with the use of the word:* "Man is a creature capable of using a dictionary" is true, but except for unusual circumstances would not be a useful trait to cite.

4. *A definition should apply to the same objects as does the word being defined:* This is the most important rule in that it touches directly upon the very function of definition, *i.e.,* to set limits on the application of a word. This rule can be broken by a definition being too narrow as when "chair" is defined as "a piece of furniture used to sit on while eating," or too broad as "a piece of furniture used to sit on." In the first case, the definition would not apply to classroom chairs and the second definition would apply to a sofa. The word being defined and the definition should be equivalent.

b) FALLACIES OF AMBIGUITY: The fallacies of ambiguity that follow are due basically to not paying attention to meaning and thus allowing premises to be irrelevant to a conclusion. When we know what the arguments mean, we can see the irrelevancy and then label the arguments with the name of a fallacy that will point to the source of the lack of clarity.

1. *Equivocation:* "All laws require a law maker, therefore, there is a law maker for the laws of nature." The ambiguous word "law" is used in two senses in this argument, consequently when this enthymeme is expanded into a syllogism there will be four terms. To make this point clear, a definition must be

constructed for each sense of the word "law." Frequently, though not necessarily, equivocation occurs within the framework of a categorical syllogism; when this is the case, it is a matter of indifference as to whether it is called equivocation or a four term fallacy.

2. *Composition:* "Every jewel in the bracelet is beautiful, therefore, the bracelet is beautiful." This argument neglects the element of structure which makes a whole other than the sum of its parts. When the meaning of the "whole object" is clarified, the ambiguity disappears and the attempt will no longer be made to "compose" an object out of its parts. This fallacy should not be confused with the inductive argument to a generalization. A generalization increases the scope of a statement in terms of quantity, whereas composition goes from all of the parts of a single entity to the whole entity.

3. *Division:* "America is a wealthy nation, therefore, every American is wealthy." This fallacy is the reverse of the fallacy of composition, and again, when the meanings of the words are clarified the ambiguity resulting from dividing a whole into its parts will disappear.

4. *Unqualified generalization:* "Hurting another person is bad, therefore, dentists commit bad acts." When the meaning of the premise is left general, the conclusion follows, but if the premise is stated more precisely the conclusion would not follow. This fallacy should not be confused with the fallacy of division since in this case a whole is not being broken into parts. The favorite occasion for making these broad unqualified generalizations is when making a moral judgment. When a person is questioned about one of these generalizations he will usually respond with "Oh, I didn't mean it in that sense."

5. *Arguing in a circle:* "Death for traitors is properly justified because it is right to put people to death who betray our country." A hasty look might indicate that something is being argued, but a closer look would show that the conclusion is merely repeating the premise in different words. The only difference between arguing in a circle and a pseudo-argument of repeated assertions is that arguing in a circle is not so blatant—the repetitions are disguised by using different words. A more obvious example of arguing in a circle is "beautiful

objects are what the experts approve of because the experts are people who approve of beautiful objects." What all of this points to is that what is to be proved is smuggled into the premises. If the question of meaning is raised, the fallacy becomes apparent.

6. *Amphiboly:* "With her eyes tightly closed, Helen knew Ruth walked over the cliff. I would conclude from this that Helen would make a very poor witness." The grammatical construction of the premise is such that it is difficult to determine whether Helen or Ruth had her eyes closed; consequently, it is impossible to tell whether the conclusion is justified.

7. *Accent:* "I guess it is all right to spend this five dollar bill. My wife only said we must start to be careful about spending pennies." By emphasizing "pennies" the argument would have some merit, but this obviously is a false accent. With a proper reading of the argument the conclusion is silly.

3. Summary

As a way of summarizing the text as well as this chapter, a complete list of fallacies, formal and non-formal, is listed below:

a) FORMAL FALLACIES

    1. *Deduction*
        1) Four terms
        2) Undistributed middle term
        3) Illicit process
        4) Affirmative premises and negative conclusion
        5) Negative premise and affirmative conclusion
        6) Two negative premises
        7) Affirming the consequent
        8) Contradicting the antecedent
        9) Affirming a disjunct in a subcontrary disjunctive syllogism
       10) Contradicting a disjunct in a contrary disjunctive syllogism

2. *Induction*
    1) Fallacy of authority
    2) Hasty generalization
    3) False analogy
    4) Post hoc

b) NON-FORMAL FALLACIES

  1. *Emotive fallacies*
    1) Ad populum
    2) Ad hominem
    3) Poisoning the well
    4) Appeal to force
    5) Argument from ignorance

  2. *Fallacies of ambiguity*
    1) Equivocation
    2) Composition
    3) Division
    4) Unqualified generalization
    5) Arguing in a circle
    6) Amphiboly
    7) Accent

EXERCISE #23: EMOTIVE FALLACIES
(For Chapter Ten, section I)

Underline the conclusions and identify each of the following emotive fallacies:

1. Medical research has failed to prove that drinking is harmful to the body; therefore, we can assume that drinking will not hurt the body.

2. There is no sense in getting fancy in our arguments. We are all plain folks and can see that Communism is bad and therefore all Communists should be eliminated.

3. Gauguin's paintings must be bad. Didn't he leave his wife and run off to the islands?

4. Naturally Mr. Jones would say that there should be a tariff on Swiss watches but he is wrong. Mr. Jones is the owner of an American watch factory.

5. Those kids must be shown that they have no right to play in the playground. We have more kids than they have and our gang has tougher fellows.

6. John is a very poor student but he should be given a passing grade. After all, his parents are sacrificing a great deal to send him to college and it would break their hearts to have him flunk out.

7. We must invade Slobovia and rescue our American boys. It hurts me deep down inside to think of those noble sons of our sweet silver-haired mothers rotting on that foreign soil.

8. Mr. Sparrow's argument against having a branch of the state university in our city is a poor one. This is obvious since he is the president of a private college in our city.

9. The psychoanalysts have failed to show that their subject has a scientific base, therefore, it is clear that it must lack such a base.

10. That rule is unfair to the students. The entire student body is against it and after all, they pay the bills. Where would the school be if the students left?

EXERCISE #24: DEFINITION
(For Chapter Ten, section II)

Criticize the following definitions in terms of the criteria of a good definition:

1. A circle is a figure whose radii are equal.

2. A good person is a person who does what is right.

3. Time is the moving image of eternity.

4. An angora cat is a cat that is very expensive.

5. A co-ed is a woman attending a school of higher learning.

6. A beautiful object is one which possesses formal design and is pleasing to the eye.

7. A good act is one that produces the most pleasure to the most people.

8. A fanatic is a man who redoubles his efforts after he has forgotten his aim.

9. A human being is a creature who can drive an airplane.

10. Temperance is the habit of foregoing present pleasure for the sake of a future greater good.

11. A woman is a bit of heaven with an apron on.

12. A star is a stellar body seen in the heavens at night.

13. Democracy is a government in which all the people vote.

14. Propaganda means any attempt to influence the opinions of others.

15. A dog is a domesticated animal having four legs.

16. A moral man is a man who is good.

17. A cynic is one who knows the price of everything and the value of nothing.

18. A lie is a locution deliberately antithetical to a verity apprehended by the intellect.

19. A painting is a picture drawn on canvas with a brush.

20. Alimony means when two people make a mistake and one of them continues to pay for it.

EXERCISE #25: FALLACIES OF AMBIGUITY
(For Chapter Ten, section II)

Underline the conclusions and identify each of the following fallacies of ambiguity:

1. Since saving is good for the individual it must be good for the nation.

2. This class is the most interesting class I have ever known; therefore, each student in the class is an interesting person.

3. Some dogs have shaggy ears. My dog has shaggy ears. Therefore, my dog is some dog.

4. We should live up to our promises, hence divorce is wrong.

5. We had better warn Hercules since the prophet said that "Hercules the dragon will slay."

6. Those men seem to be walking very carefully; so I needn't slow down for them. After all, I was only told to watch out for careless pedestrians.

7. All of my acts are good because they are all virtuous.

8. These men are cannibals. You heard them say that as they were eating a young man the son of the king came in.

9. Since the teacher told us not to ask any more questions about the marks given on the final examination it should be all right to get somebody from another class to ask the questions.

10. I have a right to criticize the present administration. I have an obligation to do what is right. Therefore, I have an obligation to criticize the present administration.

11. Whatever is the cause of evil is itself an evil. Religion has caused much evil in the world, such as wars and persecution. So religion is an evil thing.

12. Finland pays its debts, therefore the citizens of Finland pay their debts.

13. All works of art are realistic because if a work of art isn't realistic, it isn't really a work of art.

14. Mrs. J. W. Ikerman, of the Ways and Means Committee, poured the tea over a lovely lace covered table. Butterfingers!

15. The C.I.O. is a strong union so all of the members are strong.

EXERCISE #26: REVIEW OF NON-FORMAL FALLACIES
(For Chapter Ten)

Underline the conclusions and identify each of the following non-formal fallacies:

1. He who necessarily lies or necessarily tells the truth is not a free agent. But you must necessarily lie or tell the truth. Therefore, you are not a free agent.

2. Since if I got an "A" it would help me and if my girl got an "A" it would help her, it seems that if everyone in the school got an "A" it would help everyone.

3. This poem is a great poem. Therefore, every line in the poem is a great line.

4. It is good to give to a person what belongs to a person. This gun belongs to the drunk who is asking for it, therefore, I should give the gun to him.

5. It was the correct thing to do when I drained the glass. Didn't you hear the minister say "drink ye all of it?"

6. I guess it was all right for me to holler and scream because the teacher said she did not want to hear another word out of anyone.

7. "In the United States, our monetary system is unstable. Every few years it oscillates from boom to depression and back again. As our civilization grows, the oscillation becomes more violent and affects more people." This kind of assertion is un-American and hence false.

8. How can you believe him when he says teachers are underpaid? Don't you know that he is a teacher?

9. Professor Amour must be wrong. After all, he drinks, smokes, and runs around with women.

10. Material objects must exist. Have you ever known anyone who has proved that they don't exist?

11. Don't argue with me, young man. You must be wrong. Remember who pays your salary.

12. The event is so unlikely that extremely good testimony is needed before it could be accepted. And where could you get such testimony? Anyone who would testify to such nonsense is obviously a poor authority.

13. It is my duty to do unto others what I would have them do unto me: if I couldn't answer an examination question I would like my neighbor to help, therefore I should help the person next to me who seems stuck.

14. Since all intelligent men only believe consistent statements, the man who changes his mind is not intelligent.

15. Socialized Medicine is wrong for us because it is not the right way to handle our health problem.

16. It is clear that the defenders of a public health insurance bill have failed to prove that this will improve the health of the nation. From this it follows that such a bill will not improve the nation's health.

17. How can Joe's argument for Communism be correct? We all know that the reason for joining the Communist party is that a person is neurotic and is seeking for a father substitute, *i.e.,* something that will tell him what to do and will give him a sense of security.

18. What shall a person do if he is faced with the choice of

starving to death or eating food that belongs to somebody else? I say he should starve to death. Doesn't the Bible say "thou shalt not steal"?

19. The American people are against war. Do you think that, if put to a vote, the mothers of the United States of America should like to see their sons sent across the seas and slaughtered in the European dogfight?

20. A crust of bread is better than nothing and nothing is better than true love; therefore, a crust of bread is better than true love.

EXERCISE #27: REVIEW OF TEXT

For each of the following pieces of discourse: 1) if there is no argument, write assertion; 2) if there is a non-formal fallacy, write the name of the fallacy and underline or write out the conclusion; 3) if there is an inductive argument, name the type, underline or write out the conclusion and criticize the argument in terms of the appropriate criteria; 4) if there is a deductive argument, rewrite it in standard form or in symbols (use A, B, C, etc.) and evaluate it by the appropriate method:

1. Narcotics are bad, hence doctors should not use morphine on their patients.

2. It is likely that John was the one who stole the final examination because he was flunking the course up to the time of the final, he got a good grade on the final examination, his fingerprints were on the cabinet in which the final examination was kept, and he had no alibi for the time when the test was taken.

3. The name "objects" will be reserved for subject-matter so far as it has been produced and ordered in settled form by means of inquiry.

4. Since it is impossible to prove that John is guilty, there being no direct evidence against him, we may rest assured in the confident belief that he is innocent.

5. It is clear that if Joan studied diligently her teachers would regard her favorably. Since Joan is the most highly regarded person in school so far as the teachers are concerned, it must be that she studies very diligently.

6. All of the customs that exist are right and good. There can be no question about this since the writings of all of the leading sociologists take this point of view.

7. How can you believe that person? His view that we should always try to do what is good must be false. After all, he used to be a drunkard, he has been in jail, and right now he owes his ex-wife six months alimony.

8. The very best musicians in the country are in the N.B.O. Symphony Orchestra. It must be the best symphony orchestra in the country.

9. All democratically run labor unions are efficiently managed. All labor unions that have been in existence a short time are weak. No efficiently managed labor unions are weak. Therefore, no democratically run labor unions have been in existence a short time.

10. Just as waves progressively engulf a swimmer, so the objections you raise threaten to destroy the definition of the true state we have finally arrived at.

11. Hydrogen combines with oxygen because they have the proper valences to make the combination.

12. He is an accomplished pianist. Whatever is accomplished is all through. Hence he is all through as a pianist.

13. We have all heard Mr. Jones argue that the vote should be given to men who are eighteen years old. Don't listen to him. His argument is worthless. The reason for his stand is that he is eighteen years old.

14. Had he married a beautiful woman he would have been jealous, and had he married an ugly woman he would have been disgusted. Had he been either jealous or disgusted he would have been unhappy. He was not unhappy. Therefore, he did not marry a beautiful woman nor did he marry an ugly one.

15. War is evil, crime is evil and the same is true of poverty.

16. Naturally I consider him a good person. He is kind to his mother, isn't he, and only persons unkind to their mothers are bad persons.

17. It is clear that the Mayor is doing a good job in office. Why? Because he has seven children, he plays softball, and he always says hello to people he meets in the street.

18. Public Bill #1118 is a bad bill and should be defeated. This bill would give dental technicians the right to fit people with false teeth. If you had appendicitis, would you see a well trained physician and surgeon or a medical technician?

19. During the present century, every Democratic administration has seen the advent of bitter and costly wars. During Wilson's regime it was the First World War; during Franklin Roosevelt's it was the Second World War; and during Truman's second term, the Korean conflict. If you wish our country to be continuously involved in an unending series of wars, be sure to vote Democratic!

20. Since all Communists read the Daily Worker and Sidney reads the Daily Worker too, it is natural to think that Sidney is a Communist.

21. There is no doubt about it. The Nazi party members were incapable of thinking for themselves. Why I remember a time when a party member was told to deliver a message to a certain General. Even though he discovered the General was a traitor he still delivered the message to him.

22. Mental telepathy is a very puzzling phenomenon. Imagine a person in one room knowing what a person in another room is thinking about! I think I have an explanation for it though. There is a kind of immaterial entity that is completely undetectable, and this entity goes from one person to another.

23. If the teller or the cashier had pushed the alarm button, the vault would have locked automatically and the police would have arrived within three minutes. Had the police arrived within three minutes, the robber's car would have been overtaken. But the robber's car was not overtaken. Therefore, the teller did not push the alarm button.

24. Bill Allen met Bob Sullivan Sunday night, station to station, and came out a poor second. According to my survey based on 100 completed telephone calls made to numbers picked at random from both the suburban and city directories, Sullivan had 33 viewers to Allen's 18.

25. All Christians are virtuous because nobody is really a Christian unless he is virtuous.

26. The performance of Beethoven's "Eroica" was terrible. This is clear because it had no merit at all and was very badly done.

27. Philosophers are useless to the rest of the world but this is not their fault but rather because the world will not use their talents.

28. This latest victory runs the record up to three wins out of four convertible competitions entered so far by Flash V8. That's proof of Flash's hair-trigger reflexes and sure-fire handling qualities—things that make for safer, happier driving out on the road.

29. If Long's careful planning and a knowledge of human nature counts for anything, Eden's Plaza will be open for business May 19th as scheduled.

30. Herford University is the greatest university in the world, therefore its philosophy department is the greatest in the world.

31. Joe must be a varsity player because he is wearing a school letter.

32. If a person studies each course equally then he will get low grades in all of them, and if a person studies some courses enough to make high grades in them then he will fail his other courses. Either a person studies each course equally or he studies some enough to make high grades in them. Therefore, a person will either get low grades in all of his courses or he will fail some of his courses.

33. "I represent the alumni view on the problem of discrimination and of course our solution is correct. Just remember who buys the furniture for the fraternity chapter room."

34. Since the teacher said he doesn't want anybody to come in one minute late, it must be all right to come in a half hour late.

35. This is a very immoral cook book. It says to serve the meat when thoroughly stewed.

APPENDIX:

THREE TOPICS IN DEDUCTION

For the practical purpose of evaluating arguments, the material on deduction included in the text is sufficient for most situations; however, there are other topics that demand discussion both for the sake of theoretic understanding and in the interest of completeness. The purpose of this appendix is to discuss three of these topics.

1. Alternative methods for evaluating the categorical syllogism

The rules we have used for evaluating the categorical syllogism are generally regarded as the most useful tool for this purpose. There are, however, other methods in common use that have their special virtues. Three of these methods will be given a brief presentation.

a) EVALUATION BY VALID FORMS: Though this method was popular in the Middle Ages when logic occupied a major part of the time of the student, today we have gone to less cumbersome methods of evaluation. Nevertheless, it is well to have some acquaintance with this method since "form" is the key word in any discussion of validity.

1. *Technical terms:* The major term is the predicate of the conclusion, the minor term is the subject of the conclusion, the major premise is the premise that contains the major term, and the minor premise is the premise that contains the minor term. The word "mood" refers to the kinds of standard form categorical propositions that make up the syllogism and by "figure" is meant the position of the middle term. The first figure has the middle term first in the major premise and second in the minor premise; the second figure is where the middle term is second in both premises; the third figure has the middle term first in both premises; and in the fourth

figure the middle term is second in the major premise and first in the minor premise. Stating a syllogism with the major premise first and the minor premise second, any syllogism can be completely described by stating its mood and figure. For example, the syllogism "all men are mortal, and Socrates is a man, hence Socrates is mortal," would be described as "AAA-1."

2. *Valid forms:* There are 256 possible forms but after an intuitive inspection of clear examples, only 24 turn out to be valid. Testing an argument by the use of valid forms is simply a matter of comparing the argument with the list of valid forms. If the argument has the same form as one of the 24 on the list below it is valid; if it does not, then it is invalid. For example, the following argument has the form AAA-2 and hence is invalid: "all communists are equalitarians and all liberals are equalitarians, hence all liberals are communists."

AAA-1	AOO-2	OAO-3	AEE-4
EAE-1	EAE-2	AII-3	IAI-4
AII-1	AEE-2	IAI-3	EIO-4
EIO-1	EIO-2	EIO-3	AA1-4
AAI-1	AEO-2	EAO-3	EAO-4
EAO-1	EAO-2	AAI-3	AEO-4

b) EVALUATION BY VENN DIAGRAMS: The nineteenth century British logician, John Venn, discovered that by drawing a diagram with circles to represent the premises of a categorical syllogism, the conclusion will appear in the diagram if the argument is valid and it won't appear if the argument is invalid.

1. *Diagram of standard form categorical propositions:* Letting "A" stand for the subject class and "B" for the predicate class, the procedure is to draw two overlapping circles and then fill them in so that the resulting diagram will picture the meaning of the proposition.

"All A is B." The circles show that all of the subject class (the clear part of the subject circle) is in the predicate circle.

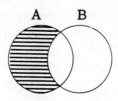

"No A is B." The circles show that none of the subject class (the clear part of the subject circle) is in the predicate class.

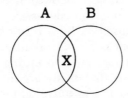

"Some A is B." The circles show that there is at least one member of the subject class (the X) that is in the predicate class.

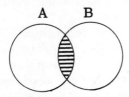

"Some A is not B." The circles show that there is at least one member of the subject class (the X) that is not in the predicate class.

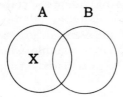

2. *Diagram of arguments:* The procedure is to first dra
three overlapping circles and label each circle with a lette
standing for each of the three terms of the argument; secon
diagram each premise (do the universal first if there is a un
versal and a particular premise); third, observe whether th
conclusion is contained in the diagram—if it is, the argumer
is valid; if it isn't, the argument is invalid. It should b
noticed that some arguments that would be valid accordin
to the rules and valid forms are invalid when tested by th
Venn diagrams. Specifically, these would be the last two vali
forms in each of the first three figures and the last three form
in the fourth figure. An example would be the diagram o
the fifth argument below.

What these forms have in common is that they move fror
two universal premises to a particular conclusion. The reaso
for calling this kind of argument invalid is to disallow a
argument like the following: "all dragons are fire-breather
and all fire-breathers are maiden-eaters, hence some dragon
are maiden-eaters." The argument begins with universa
premises that clearly do not intend the real existence of th
object referred to, but the particular conclusion sounds as i
there really are dragons. Because of this situation, the Venu
diagrams regard universal propositions as merely hypothetica
while particular propositions do assert existence and use ar
"X" to symbolize existence. This being the case, it would b
invalid to move from universal premises to a particular con
clusion. The reason for our not adding a rule to this effec
in our list of rules is that many arguments in everyday dis
course do intend existence by universal propositions.

The following argument would be called valid in any
normal situation: "all collies are dogs and all collies are ani
mals, hence some animals are dogs." It is a matter of arbitrar
choice whether to call this argument invalid unless there is a
proposition added saying "there are collies," or to call it valic
and add that you are assuming "there are collies." Five ex
amples of the use of the Venn diagrams follow; it should be
observed that in the fourth example, where there is a choice a
to where to put the "X," it is placed on a line.

        A   B

1) All dogs are animals

        C   A

All collies are dogs

            C   B

Hence, all collies are animals.

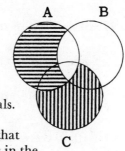

    Valid—the circles show that
    all of the "C" left clear is in the
    "B," *i.e.,* all collies are animals.

        A   B

2) All dogs are animals

        C   B

All cats are animals

            C   A

Hence, all cats are dogs.

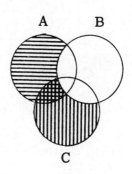

    Invalid—part of the
    "C" left clear is in the
    "B," *i.e.,* it is not true
    that all cats are dogs.

        A   B

3) All dogs are animals

        A   C

Some dogs are hunters

            C   B

Hence, some hunters are animals.

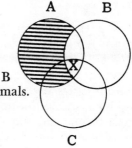

    Valid—the "X" shows that
    there is at least one "C"
    that is in the "B," *i.e.,*
    some hunters are animals.

      A   B

4) All collies are dogs

      C   B

Some animals are dogs

      C   A

Hence, some animals are collies.

> Invalid—the "X" shows
> that there may be a "C" that
> is in the "A" but there need
> not be. It is not necessarily
> true that some animals are collies.

      A   B

5) All collies are dogs

      A   C

All collies are animals

      C   B

Hence, some animals are dogs.

> Invalid—the conclusion
> asserts there is an "X" but no
> "X" appears on the diagram. If
> there are collies then some animals
> are dogs, but the premises do not
> tell us that there are collies.

c) <u>EVALUATION BY AN ANTILOGISM</u>: The method we will us
and it is a very simple and effective device, is the abbreviatio
of the Ladd-Franklin method formulated by Professor Delto
Howard. An antilogism is constructed out of a syllogism l
contradicting the conclusion. The test of validity consists .
applying the following two rules to the antilogism: (1) The
must be one and only one negative proposition. (2) Every ter
must be distributed at least once. If both rules are obeyed, t
original argument is valid; if not, the argument is invalid. T
antilogism will correspond to the Venn diagrams if one mo
rule is added: there must be one particular proposition. Tv
examples of the use of this method follow:

1) All dogs are animals
   All collies are dogs
   Hence, all collies are animals.

> Contradict conclusion to "some collies are
> not animals" and we find one negative
> proposition and each term distributed at
> least once, hence the original argument
> is valid.

2) All dogs are animals
   No cats are dogs
   Hence, no cats are animals.

> Contradict conclusion to "some cats are animals"
> and we find one negative proposition but we also
> discover that "animals" is not distributed, hence
> the original argument is invalid.

2. Intertranslation of categorical and compound arguments

The text has treated categorical and compound arguments as two separate species, each with its own tests of validity, but the question could be raised as to whether one method could be used to evaluate both kinds of arguments. From the practical viewpoint of evaluating arguments, it is probably easiest to work with both methods, however, from the theoretic point of view it would be simpler to operate with one method if this is possible. There has been an extensive discussion among logicians about the possibility of a reduction to one method with one side saying that it would involve a loss of meaning and the other side, and this is the dominant position, claiming that Aristotelian logic is merely a part of symbolic logic and can be reduced to symbolic logic. Without arguing this matter, we will give a brief and hence somewhat incomplete indication of how such a reduction is made.

a) SAMPLE TRANSLATION SITUATIONS: The first argument listed below is easily translated with the tools we already possess, but the second and third arguments present new problems.

1. *Categorical argument with all general universal proposi-tions:* "All dogs are animals, all collies are dogs, hence all

collies are animals." This argument can be verbally translated as "if a thing is a dog then it is an animal; if a thing is a collie then it is a dog, hence if a thing is a collie then it is an animal." The argument can then be symbolized and proved as follows

1. A ⊃ B
2. C ⊃ A / C ⊃ B
3. C ⊃ B 2,1; P ⊃ Q, Q ⊃ R / P ⊃ R

2. *Categorical arguments with singular propositions:* The argument "all collies are dogs, Lassie is a collie, hence Lassie is a dog," might on impulse be translated into "if a thing is a collie then it is a dog; Lassie is a collie, hence Lassie is a dog." The difficulty arises when an attempt is made to symbolize the latter argument. To write it as "A ⊃ B, A, hence B" is not correct because the "A" in the first premise stands for "a thing is a collie" whereas the "A" in the second premise would stand for "Lassie is a collie."

3. *Categorical arguments with particular propositions:* "All collies are dogs, some collies are heroes, hence some heroes are dogs." An attempt to translate and symbolize this argument in the compound idiom runs into immediate failure. For this argument as for the one above, what seems needed is a new technique of symbolization that will take quantity into account.

b) QUANTIFIED SYMBOLIC LOGIC: By a quantified symbolic logic is meant a technique of symbolizing that will make distinctions between general universal propositions, singular universal propositions, and particular propositions. With this added apparatus, the last two arguments above can be handled by symbolic logic.

1. *Universal quantification:* When we translated "all collies are dogs" into compound form it turned out to be "if a thing is a collie then it is a dog" and it was symbolized as "A ⊃ B." We will now word the translation "for any thing, if the thing is a collie then the thing is a dog," and let the quantifier "x" stand for "thing." The resulting symbolization would be "(x) Ax ⊃ Bx," and it would be read " for any x, if x is an A, then x is a B." It is customary to place the "x," the symbol for the entity

that has a property, behind the "A" and "B" that symbolize the properties of being a collie and being a dog.

2. *Particular quantification:* A particular proposition such as "some collies are heroes" is interpreted as asserting the existence of at least one individual that is a collie and is a hero. The symbol "Ex" will be used to symbolize an existent "x." The complete symbolization of the above proposition would then be "(Ex) Ax . Bx" and it would be read as "there is an x such that x is a collie and x is a hero."

3. *Singular quantification:* A singular proposition such as "Lassie is a collie" again asserts existence but this time the existence is of a specific individual. The symbol "Ei" is used to stand for a specific existing individual and the complete symbolization of the above proposition would be "(Ei) Ax . Bx." This expression can be read as "there is a specific individual that is Lassie and is a collie."

c) SOLUTION OF THE TWO PROBLEM CASES: We are now in a position to indicate how categorical arguments with singular or particular propositions can be translated into compound arguments, symbolized, and evaluated.

1. *Categorical arguments with particular propositions:* Our example will be the one that caused our earlier trouble, namely, "all collies are dogs, some collies are heroes, hence some heroes are dogs." A verbal translation would be "for any x if x is a collie then x is a dog; there is an x such that it is a collie and a hero, hence there is an x such that it is a hero and a dog." The symbolization and proof would be:

1. (x) Ax ⊃ Bx
2. (Ex) Ax . Cx / (Ex) Cx . Bx
3. Ax 2; P . Q / P
4. Bx 1,3; P ⊃ Q, P / Q
5. Cx 2; P . Q / Q
6. Cx . Bx 5,4; P, Q / P . Q

2. *Categorical arguments with singular propositions:* There is no need to elaborate the explanation of how this kind of argument could be handled by symbolic logic since the procedure could be the same as for arguments with particular

propositions. The only possible difference would be that a singular proposition could be symbolized in briefer fashion if this would be helpful in the proof. Thus, in the argument "all collies are dogs, Lassie is a collie, hence Lassie is a dog," the proposition "Lassie is a collie" could be symbolized as "(Ei) Ax" and read as "there is an individual named Lassie that is a collie." The complete symbolization of the argument would be:

$$(x) \ Ax \supset Bx$$
$$(Ei) \ Ax \ / \ (Ei) \ Bx$$

3. Deductive systems

By a deductive system is meant a body of propositions some of which are premises that are not proved in the system and the remainder are conclusions that are implied by the premises. A specific example of a deductive system is Euclid's geometry; here we find a set of initial propositions and then a series of theorems or conclusions that are deduced. The aim of such a system is to start with the fewest possible premises and still prove all of the conclusions in the system. Instead of starting with a rather eclectic list of premises as we did with our list of valid forms and logical equivalences, it is theoretically more satisfying to start with a list that can't be proved and then add to the list by proving other propositions. We will begin our discussion by showing how the system used in the section on symbolic logic did not start with the fewest possible premises, *i.e.*, the shortest possible list of valid forms and logical equivalences, and we will go on to make explicit the total set of elements involved in any deductive system but with specific reference to symbolic logic.

a) REDUNDANCY OF THE LIST OF VALID FORMS AND LOGICAL EQUIVALENCES: There were several occasions when it was implicitly stated that the list of valid forms and logical equivalences could have been reduced in number without affecting our ability to evaluate arguments. It was clear at certain points that we could use some forms to prove other forms. The advantage of the longer list is that it gives more to work with, and hence proofs can be constructed more easily. To take one example, the following argument could simply be labeled valid on the basis of our list, but if the form "P ⊃ Q, ∼Q / ∼P" were eliminated, the argument could be proved as indicated.

1. A ⊃ B
2. ∼B / ∼A
3. ∼B ⊃ ∼A 1; P ⊃ Q ≡ ∼Q ⊃ ∼P
4. ∼A 3, 2; P ⊃ Q, P / Q

For the same reasons, we could eliminate valid forms #4, #6, and #10. Also, since there are equivalences between the various kinds of compound propositions, it would be possible to make an arbitrary choice and eliminate, for example, #1 and #3. Using form #5 and equivalences we could easily prove the following argument:

1. A ⊃ B
2. A / B
3. ∼(A . ∼B) 1; P ⊃ Q ≡ ∼(P . ∼Q)
4. B 3,2; ∼(P . Q), P / ∼Q

It is a difficult task to reduce a deductive system to a minimum of premises, but it is clear that the redundancies noted above could be eliminated. Are there any others? Another way of asking this question is to ask whether any of the remaining valid forms and equivalences could be proved. If one can be proved, then it is not a premise.

b) ELEMENTS OF A DEDUCTIVE SYSTEM: In a general way, the elements are the premises and conclusions; however, this classification can be broken down into the following finer ingredients:

1. *Primitive notions:* There is a wide range of choice as to what ideas to start with, but the following three offer an indication of what might be done: 1) A proposition will be represented by the symbols "P, Q, R, etc." 2) A rule of combination of the symbols is given by a dot (".") so that "P . Q" means both propositions are true. 3) Negation is symbolized by a curl ("∼") so that "∼P" means "P is false."

2. *Definitions:* We can now introduce new symbols to facilitate deductions by defining them in terms of the primitive notions. The symbol "=" means "by definition."

1) $P \supset Q = \sim(P . \sim Q)$
2) $P \lor Q = \sim(\sim P . \sim Q)$
3) $P \equiv Q = (P \supset Q) . (Q \supset P)$

3. *Postulates or basic premises:* By inspecting our primitive notions and definitions we can see that certain propositions must be true:

1) $P \supset (P \lor Q)$
2) $(P \lor Q) \supset (Q \lor P)$
3) $(P . Q) \supset (Q . P)$

4. *Theorems:* Using primitive notions, definitions, and postulates a number of theorems can be proved. After a theorem has been proved, it can then be used in proofs of other theorems. An example of a proof of a theorem would be:

To be proved: $(P \supset Q) \supset (\sim Q \supset \sim P)$

Proof: 1. $\sim(P . \sim Q) \supset \sim(\sim Q . P)$
                       by third postulate

                  2. $(P \supset Q) \supset (\sim Q \supset \sim P)$
                       by first definition

What has been done in this proof is first to turn the disjunctive proposition around on the basis of an evident postulate. The second step consists in using the first definition to show that the proposition to be proved is an exact substitution for the proposition in step number one.

INDEX